Editors
Rebecca Wood
Erica N. Russikoff, M.A.

Illustrator
Clint McKnight

Cover Artists
Kevin Barnes
Barb Lorseyedi

Editor in Chief
Ina Massler Levin, M.A.

Creative Director
Karen J. Goldfluss, M.S. Ed.

Art Coordinator
Renée Christine Yates

Imaging
Rosa C. See

Publisher
Mary D. Smith, M.S. Ed.

Puzzles and Games That Make Kids **Think**

Grade 6

Over **175** activities that:
• enhance critical thinking
• encourage problem solving
• engage curious minds

Author

Garth Sundem, M.M.

Teacher Created Resources, Inc.
6421 Industry Way
Westminster, CA 92683
www.teachercreated.com

ISBN: 978-1-4206-2566-0

© 2009 Teacher Created Resources, Inc.
Made in U.S.A.

Teacher Created Resources

Table of Contents

Table of Contents *(cont.)*

Introduction

Welcome to *Puzzles and Games That Make Kids Think*. This book contains over 185 puzzles and games of more than 30 different types, each of which is not only fun, but also asks students to use their minds to figure out the solution. (There are no "word finds" here!) Students will find some of these puzzles difficult while other puzzles will be easy. Some puzzles will take seconds, while others might take half an hour. All of the puzzles are a workout for the brain! Here are a few reasons why we think you'll enjoy this book:

- Puzzle-based brain workouts create results. Research shows that a regimen of brainteasers can lead to higher scores on problem-solving tests.[1] Research also shows that using puzzles in the classroom can lead to increased student interest and involvement.[2]

- There are four categories of brainteasers in this book: picture, word, number, and logic, with puzzles (for individual students) and games (for pairs) for each category. Within each section, students will use diverse thinking skills—in a picture puzzle, students may draw lines on a geometric figure, and in a number puzzle, they may need to read complex directions. The wide variety of puzzles keeps students engaged and entertained.

- Each page of this book includes all of the needed directions and materials (other than writing utensils!), making it easy to distribute these puzzles to early finishers. Or, you may choose to copy and distribute puzzles as part of a reward system or weekly brain-buster challenge. Students will look forward to these fun puzzles, and you can rest assured that your classroom time will be spent productively. Another use of these puzzles is to spice up homework packets—strategically insert a puzzle or two to keep things lively!

- With a less experienced class, you may need to preview puzzle directions ahead of time (especially the two-person games and logic puzzles). Consider exploring the directions as a class before independent work time. Or, explain that reading and understanding the instructions is the first part of the puzzle! Because puzzle types repeat, students will gain more confidence in their ability to solve the puzzles as they spend more time with this book.

Be careful—these puzzles are addictive, and you can easily find yourself whiling away a prep period with pencil in hand!

[1] Howard, P. J. (1994). *The Owner's Manual for the Brain.* Charlotte, NC: Leornian Press.
[2] Finke, R. A., et al. (1992). *Creative Cognition: Theory, Research, and Applications.* Cambridge, MA: The MIT Press.

Puzzle Hints

Game Hints

Some games require the ability to read and understand somewhat difficult directions. Consider previewing directions with students beforehand. Also notice that some games require photocopying the page (or allowing students to cut shapes or game boards from the book). With less experienced classes, you might play a full-class version of a game (teacher versus students) before allowing pairs to work independently. In hopes of keeping game directions brief and student friendly, many of the more intuitive rules have been omitted. If students have questions about game mechanics, encourage them to use their common sense.

Picture Puzzles

- *Fit It!:* If you like, trace (or copy) and cut out the shapes.

- *Map Madness:* Make sure you start at the correct point. Then, follow the route with your finger.

- *Rebus:* Where are words and/or pictures in relation to each other or to other elements? Say these relationships aloud and listen for common phrases.

- *Shape Construction:* If you like, trace (or copy) and cut out the shapes.

- *Shape Find:* First, imagine the shape in your mind. Then, try to work around the figure systematically. And don't forget the whole figure itself!

- *Shape Slap:* Use the big shapes first. Place them in ways that will block your opponent.

- *Split Shapes:* Usually the lines are drawn from corners. Start there first.

- *What's Different?:* Pretend there is a grid over each picture, and confine your search to only one box at a time.

Word Puzzles

- *Before and After:* If it doesn't come to you right away, brainstorm words that would fit the correct number of boxes.

- *Crack the Code:* Fill in each box in order. If you're running out of time, you can usually guess the answer before finishing the last few boxes.

- *Crossword:* Do the easy ones first. Then, use those letters to help you determine the more difficult ones.

- *Hide and Seek:* Scan the sentence slowly, looking for the names of different animals.

- *Letter Scramble:* Play with the vowel—it's usually the key.

- *Transformers:* Look at the last word. Which letter from this word could be inserted in the first word to make a new word? Repeat until you get to the bottom.

Puzzle Hints (cont.)

Number Puzzles

- *Addition Tree:* If it doesn't work from the top down, try filling in the boxes from the bottom up.

- *Fill in the Blanks:* Start on the right, with the singles digit, and then work left.

- *In Addition:* If there are three numbers in any row or column, you can find the fourth number. Do those first.

- *It's Touching:* First, look for rows or columns that are missing only one number. Then, look for shaded numbers with only one blank box touching.

- *Math Path:* You will almost always add the greatest numbers. In longer puzzles, look for a path between the two greatest numbers that includes an addition sign for both.

- *Multiplication Tree:* Try filling in the boxes from the bottom up.

- *Snake Race:* Keep in mind the numbers that add up to your target number. Then, look for one of those numbers in the puzzle. Start at that number and experiment with ways to move until you find the combination you need.

- *Sudoku:* If a row or column already contains five numbers, you can fill in the sixth. Fill those in before proceeding.

- *Thinking of a Number:* Work from the filled-in digit.

Logic Puzzles

- *Apples and Oranges:* If you know how much one fruit costs, then you can figure out how much the other fruit costs.

- *Jason's Hat, Melissa's Necklace, etc.:* Memorize the three things you are looking for (e.g., + stripe, + feather, + brim in front). Then scan the puzzle in order, looking for the picture that matches the description.

- *Letter Box:* Make sure students know the definitions of *row* and *column*.

- *Mike, Anita, and Jamal:* If two people did not do something, the third must have. If someone did something, it means that no one else did it and that he or she did not do anything else. (This will help you draw **X**s on the chart.)

- *Paint by Numbers:* Start by filling in the rows with the greatest numbers. Then, you can figure out the rest by process of elimination.

- *What's Next?:* Look for the repeating pattern.

1 Rebus

These are pictures of common sayings. What are they?

_____   _____

2 Shape Find

How many triangles can you find in this picture? _____

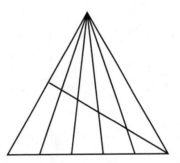

3 Shape Construction

Combine the shapes below to make a square.

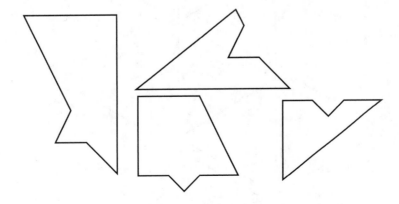

Solid Gold Game

4

Directions:

1. Find a partner, and cut out the shape below.

2. Decide who goes first.

3. Take turns: You each get 30 seconds to try to fold this shape into a solid.

4. Whoever makes the solid first wins! Tape your solid together. If you have time, play again.

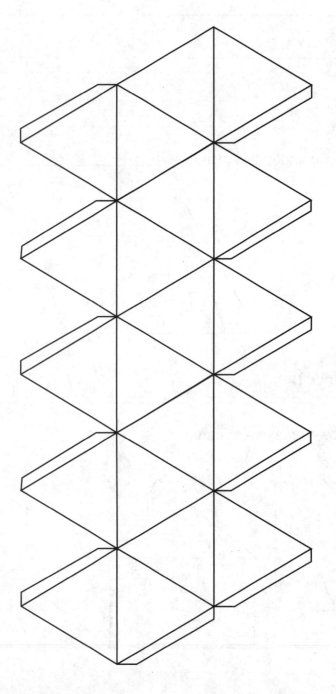

Fit It!

5

Fit all of the shapes into the square below. Either draw your answer, or trace and cut out the shapes before laying them on the square.

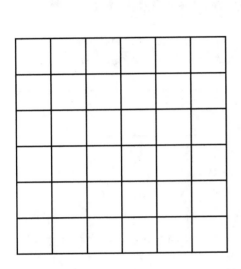

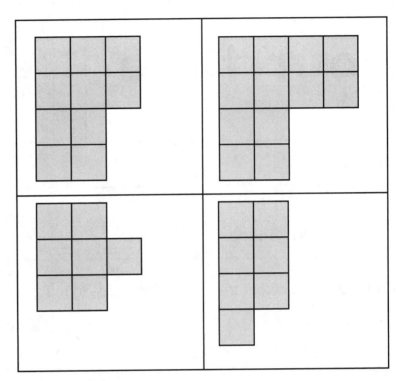

What's Different?

6

Can you spot the five differences between these two pictures? Circle them.

7 Rebus

These are representations of common sayings. What are they?

_____   _____

8 Split Shapes

Can you draw another triangle on this shape to make seven new triangles and one hexagon?

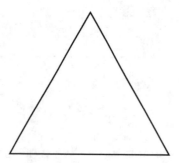

9 Shape Find

How many rectangles can you find in this picture? _____

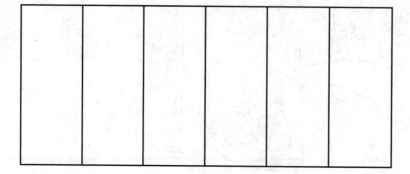

Triangle Take-Away Game

10

Directions:

1. Find a partner.

2. Put a blank piece of paper over the picture below, and trace it lightly in pencil.

3. Take turns erasing a line. You can erase a long or short line. But, you must leave at least one triangle.

4. The first person who cannot leave a triangle loses.

5. If you have time, trace the shape again and play another round!

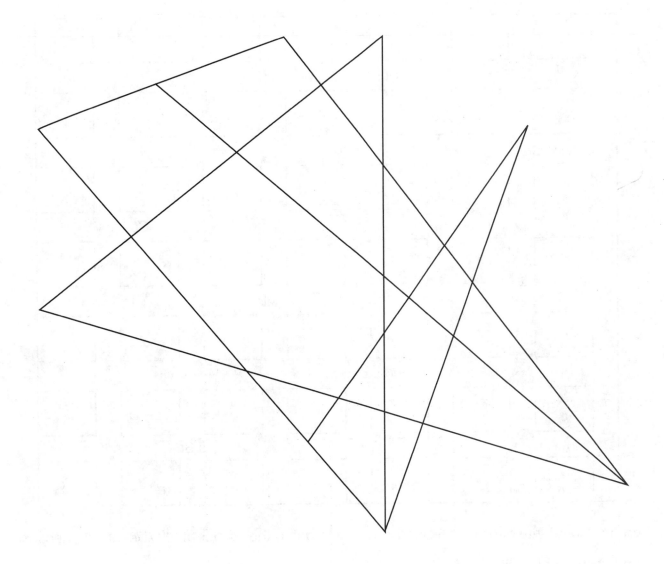

Map Madness!

11

Do you see Raul? He is lost! Follow the directions to get him back on track. Mark his ending spot with an **X**.

Directions:

1. 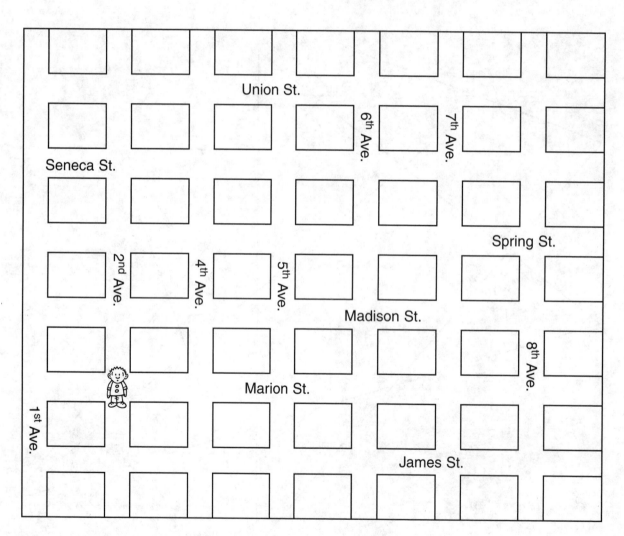 Go north on 2nd Ave.

2. Turn right on Union St.

3. Turn right on 4th Ave.

4. Turn left on Spring St.

5. Turn right on 5th Ave.

6. **END** End at the corner of James St.

Bonus: Now, write directions telling Raul how to get to the corner of 8th Ave. and Seneca St. from his current location. _____

Rebus

12

These are pictures of common sayings. What are they?

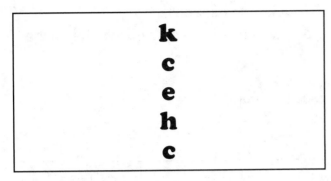

Shape Construction

13

Combine the shapes below to make a triangle.

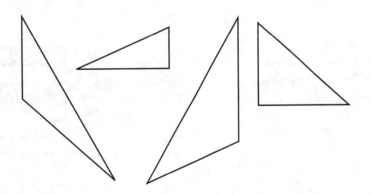

Split Shapes

14

Can you draw a square on this shape to make eight new triangles? There are two ways to do it. Can you find both ways?

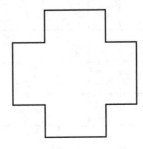

Shape Slap

15

Directions:

1. Find a partner. Look at the game board. Then, look at the shapes.
2. Pick a shape. Color in this shape on the board. If you need to, you can spin the shape. Draw an **X** over the shape you used.
3. Now, it is your partner's turn.
4. The first person who does not have room to place a shape loses.

Shapes:

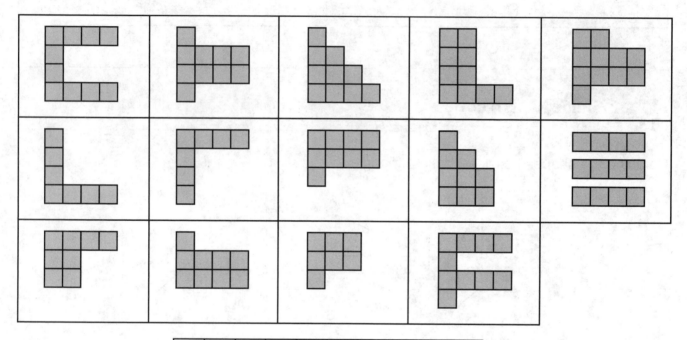

Game Board:

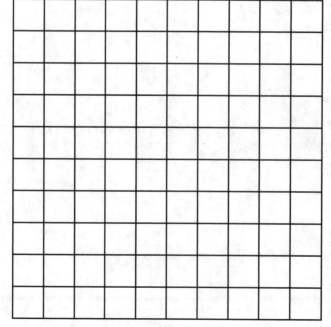

Do you see Raul? He is lost again! Follow the directions to get him back on track. Mark his ending spot with an **X**.

Directions:

1. ◀ Go west on 72nd St.

2. ▼ Go southeast on Broadway.

3. ▶ Turn right on W. 58 St.

4. ▶ Turn right on Amsterdam Ave.

5. ◀ Turn left on W. 59th St.

6. **END** End at the corner of Henry Hudson Pkwy.

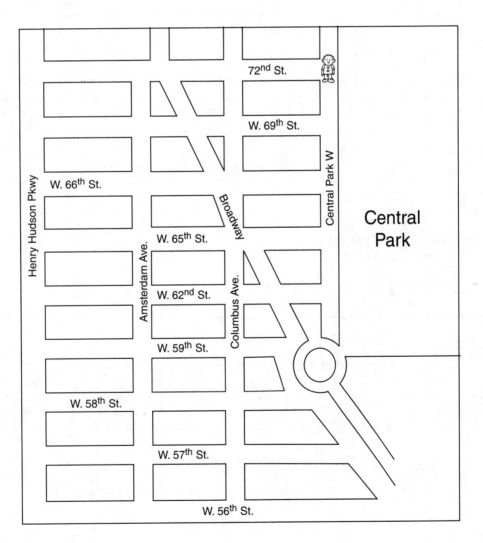

Bonus: Now, write directions telling Raul how to get to the corner of Broadway and W. 58th St. from his current location. _____

_____

Fit It!

17

Fit all of the shapes into the square below. Either draw your answer, or trace and cut out the shapes before laying them on the square.

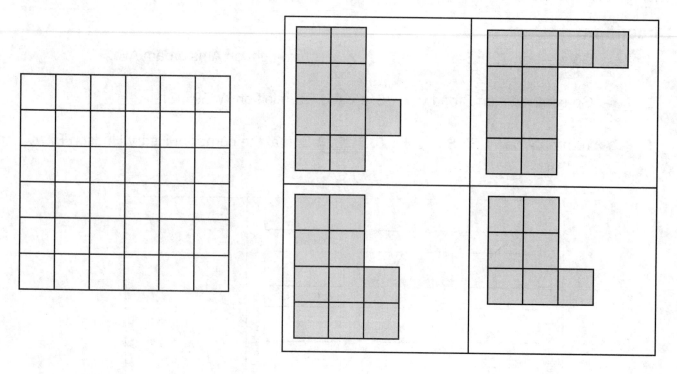

What's Different?

18

Can you spot the five differences between these two pictures? Circle them.

Joiner's Game

19

Directions:

1. Find a partner. Each of you will need a copy of this sheet with your own set of shapes. Cut out the shapes below.

2. Each of these shapes can be cut into three pieces so that you can combine them to make a square or a rectangle.

3. Race to make squares and rectangles—draw lines on your shapes until you think you have figured out which cuts will allow you to make these shapes. Then, cut out your pieces and make a square or a rectangle. Once you have drawn lines, cut your three pieces, and made a square or rectangle, the shape is closed.

4. Whoever makes the most squares and/or rectangles wins!

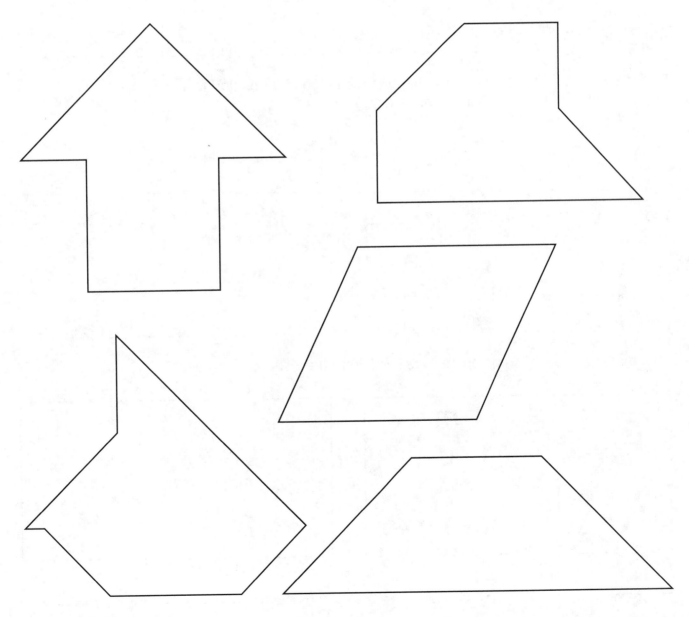

Shape Construction

20

Combine the shapes below to make a pentagon.

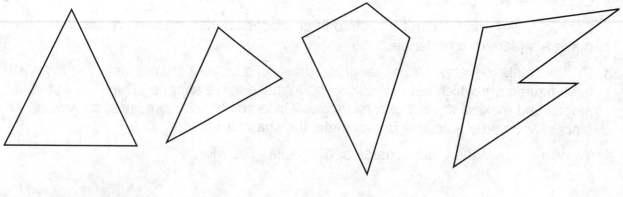

Split Shapes

21

Can you draw two squares on this shape to make ten squares and four triangles?
(*Note:* There will be other shapes remaining.)

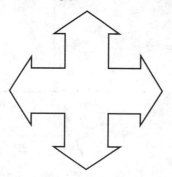

Rebus

22

These are pictures of common sayings. What are they?

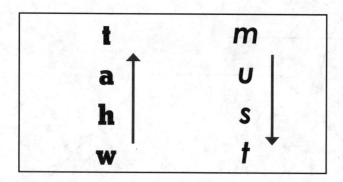

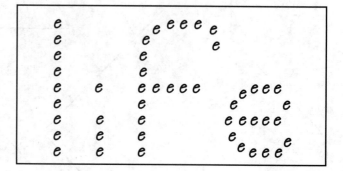

Fit It!

23

Fit all of the shapes into the square below. Either draw your answer, or trace and cut out the shapes before laying them on the square.

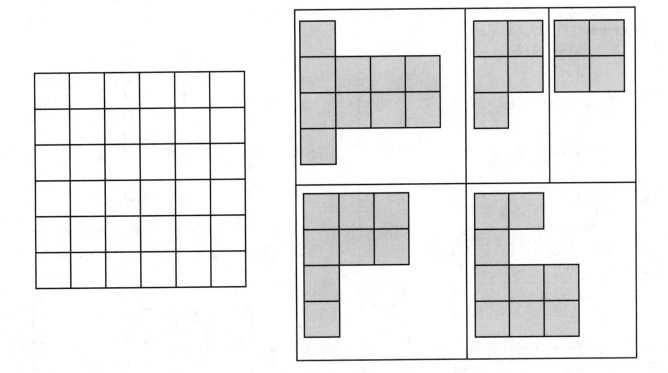

Shape Find

24

How many crescent moons (of any dimension) can you find in this picture? _____

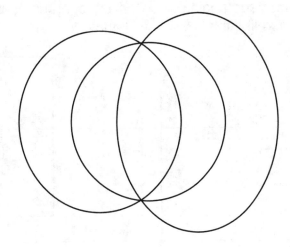

Funny Fold-Overs

25

Directions:

1. Work in a pair or in a group of three. Each player takes a sheet of paper and folds it into thirds like this:

2. Each player draws a funny head in the top third like this:

3. Now, fold back the top third of your paper so that it looks like this:

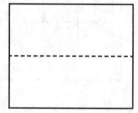

Trade pages with a partner. Your partner should not be able to see the head you drew.

4. Draw a body in the middle third like this:

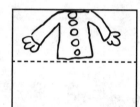

5. Fold back your paper and trade again. Draw legs in the lower third like this:

6. Now open up your drawing to see your funny person!

Do you see Raul? He is lost again! Follow the directions to get him back on track. Mark his ending spot with an **X**.

Directions:

1. Take the 101 west.

2. Take the 110 south.

3. Exit at W. 4th St., and follow it to S. Broadway.

4. Turn left on S. Broadway, and follow it as it changes to N. Broadway.

5. Turn left on W. Temple St.

6. **END** End at the corner of N. Grand Ave.

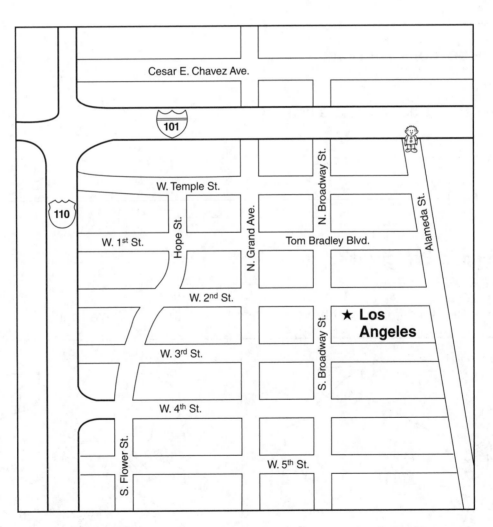

Bonus: Now, write directions telling Raul how to get to the corner of W. 5th St. and S. Flower St. from his current location. _____

_____

Rebus
27

These are pictures of common sayings. What are they?

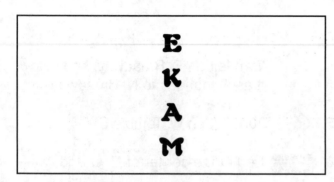

Shape Construction
28

Combine the shapes below to make an arrow.

What's Different?
29

Can you spot the five differences between these two pictures? Circle them.

Maze-Maker Game

30

Directions:

1. Find a partner.
2. Draw a maze, taking turns drawing paths. When it is your turn, you must draw a split and a dead end. Then, it is your partner's turn. Here is an example:

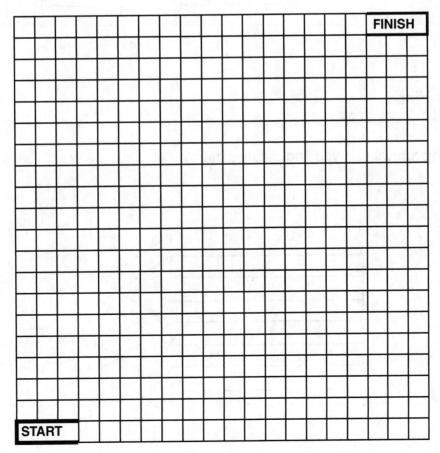

3. Continue drawing your maze until your path reaches the finish. (Try to fill the entire space!)
4. Make two photocopies of your maze. Now, it's time to solve the maze! Who can solve it the fastest? If you like, trade mazes with other pairs.

31 Fit It!

Fit all of the shapes into the square below. Either draw your answer, or trace and cut out the shapes before laying them on the square.

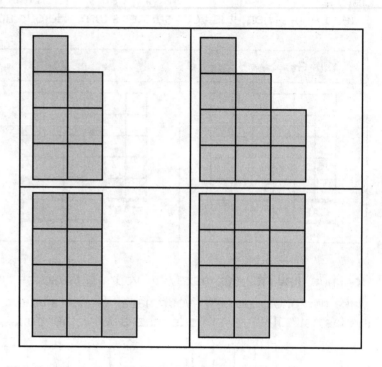

32 Shape Find

How many pointing arrows can you find in this picture? _____

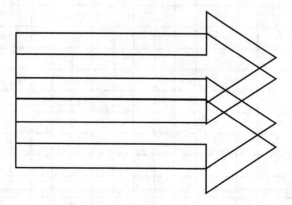

Map Madness!

Do you see Raul? He is lost again! Follow the directions to get him back on track. Mark his ending spot with an **X**.

Directions:

1. Take Hennepin Ave. southwest.

2. Turn left just after the City Shopping Center.

3. Turn left on 2nd Ave. S.

4. Go east on E. 3rd St.

5. Turn right on S. 5th Ave.

6. **END** End at the corner of S. 8th St.

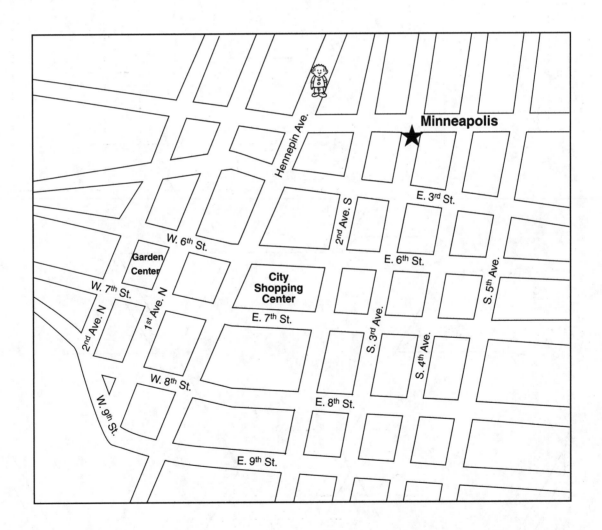

Bonus: Now, write directions telling Raul how to get to the Garden Center from his current location. _____

_____

Solid Gold Game

34

Directions:

1. Find a partner. Each of you will need a copy of this sheet. Cut out the shape below.

2. Decide who goes first.

3. Take turns. You each get 30 seconds to try to fold this shape into a solid.

4. Whoever makes the solid first wins! Tape your solid together. If you have time, play again.

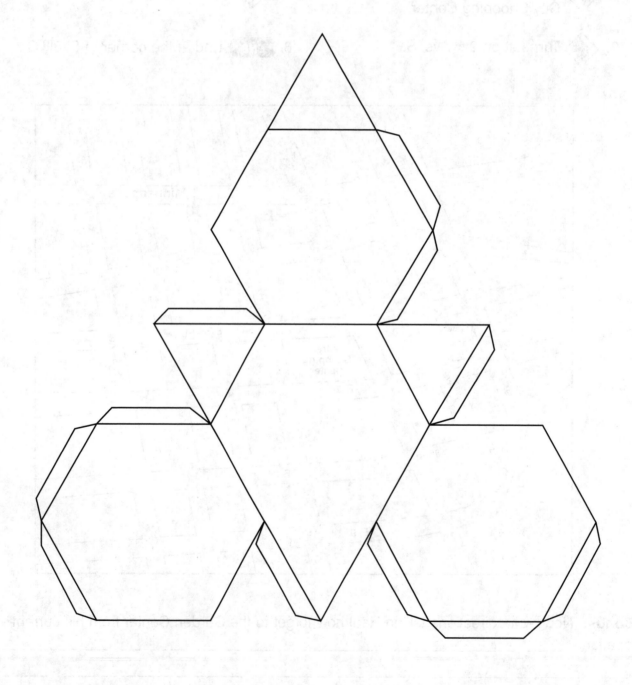

Shape Construction

35

Combine the shapes below to make a heart.

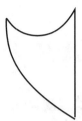 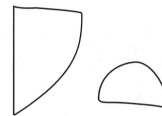

Shape Find

36

How many hearts can you find in this picture? _____

Rebus

37

These are pictures of common sayings. What are they?

sitting THE WORLD	m1llion	**Go** *it it it it*
_____	_____	_____

Rebus
38

These are pictures of common sayings. What are they?

can can	**highway** **pass**

Split Shapes
39

Can you draw two lines on this shape to make eight triangles?

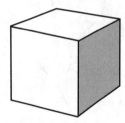

What's Different?
40

Can you spot the five differences between these two pictures? Circle them.

Shape Slap

41

Directions:

1. Find a partner. Look at the game board. Then, look at the shapes.
2. Pick a shape. Color in this shape on the board. If you need to, you can spin the shape. Draw an **X** over the shape you used.
3. Now, it is your partner's turn.
4. The first person who does not have room to place a shape loses!

Shapes:

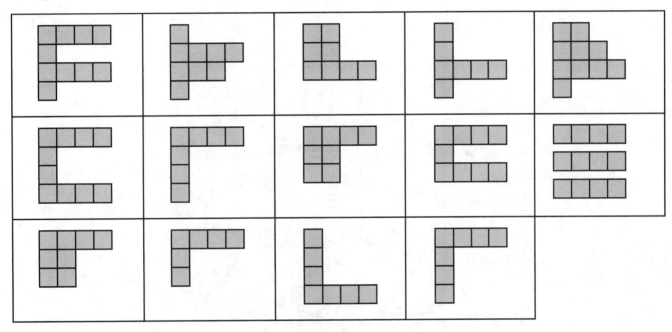

Game Board:

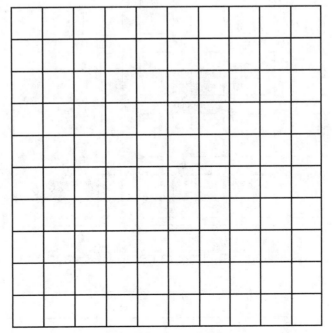

Map Madness!

Do you see Raul? He is lost again! Follow the directions to get him back on track. Mark his ending spot with an **X**.

Directions:

1. ⬆ Take Abbott St. toward Water St.

2. ⬅ Turn onto W. Cordova St. toward Howe St.

3. ⬅ Go left on Richards St.

4. ⬆ Go west on W. Georgia St.

5. ⬆ Turn onto Howe St. toward W. Hastings St.

6. ⬆ End at the corner of Dunsmuir St.

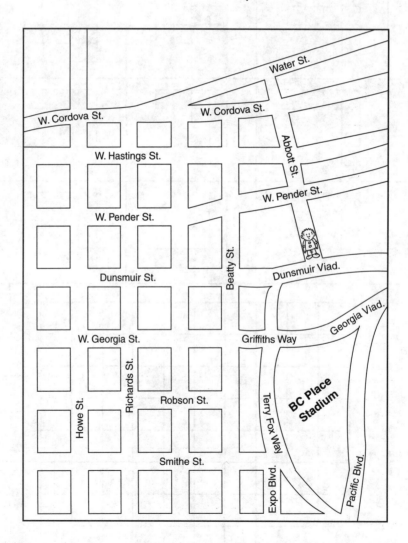

Bonus: Now, write directions telling Raul how to get to BC Place Stadium from his current location. _____

_____

Split Shapes

43

Can you draw one line on this shape to make six triangles?

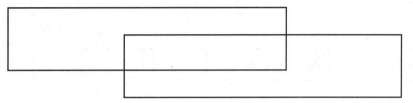

Rebus

44

These are pictures of common sayings. What are they?

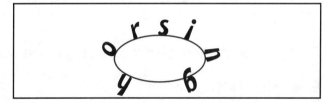

Fit It!

45

Fit all of the shapes into the square below. Either draw your answer, or trace and cut out the shapes before laying them on the square.

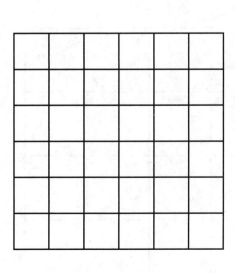

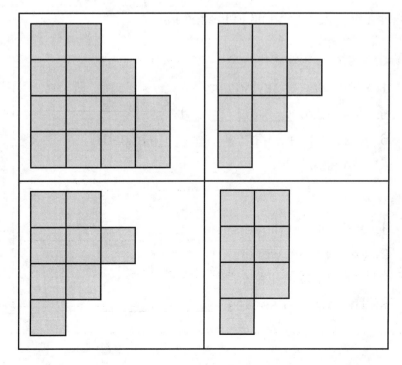

46 Before and After

Put a word in the blank boxes so that it makes a word or short phrase with the words in front and the word after.

Example:

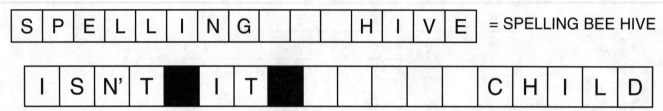

| S | P | E | L | L | I | N | G | | | H | I | V | E | = SPELLING BEE HIVE |

| I | S | N' | T | ■ | I | T | ■ | | | | | C | H | I | L | D |

47 Hide and Seek

Can you find the three animals hiding in this sentence? Circle them.

Example: Hel(p ig)loos!

Bingo attendance feels lugubrious tonight.

48 Crossword

Read the clues and fill in the letters.

Across

1. short way of saying *until*

5. I have an _____ !

6. to schedule a trip (_____ ahead)

7. to mail a letter

Down

1. ends of your fingers

2. inactive, not working

3. to rest against a wall

4. The explorer spotted _____ .

1	2	3	4
5			
6			
7			

Letter Scramble

49

Make four words using all of these letters: stac.

1. _____   3. _____

2. _____   4. _____

Hide and Seek

50

Can you find the three animals hiding in this sentence? Circle them.

Example: Help igloos!

We need a bigger billboard with the blob's terrible ooze branded on it.

Crack the Code

51

What is green and has two legs and a trunk? Fill in the blanks with these letters to find out!

o	a	i	s	k	u	i

	■	s	e	a		c	■	t		r	s	t

Make-a-Word Game

52

Directions:

1. Find a partner. You will be competing to make words.

2. Choose who goes first. This person can pick any starting letter.

3. Take turns adding one letter.

4. When you add a letter, you must have a word in mind that you are trying to spell. It doesn't need to be the same word your partner has in mind. Here is an example:

Starting letter	Player #2	Player #1	Player #2	Player #1	Player #2	#1 = Winner!
T	R	I	P	L	E	D

5. If you think your partner has added a letter without having a word in mind, you can challenge him or her. If your partner can tell you his or her word, he or she wins; if your partner just added a random letter, you win.

6. The first person who is unable to add a letter loses. If you run out of game boards, you can make more of your own.

Game Boards:

Starting Letter	2	1	2	1	2	1	2	1	2

Starting Letter	1	2	1	2	1	2	1	2	1

Starting Letter	2	1	2	1	2	1	2	1	2

Starting Letter	1	2	1	2	1	2	1	2	1

53 Hide and Seek

Can you find the four animals hiding in this sentence? Circle them.

Example: Help igloos!

Pro bingo players made lemon, Key lime pie for the fortunate cowboy.

54 Letter Scramble

Make four words using all of these letters: estn.

1. _____   3. _____

2. _____   4. _____

55 Transformers

Change one letter at a time to get from the top word to the bottom word. Each row must make a real word.

Example:

p	e	s	t
p	o	s	t
p	o	e	t
p	o	e	m

n	e	s	t
m	e	a	l

56 Hide and Seek

Can you find the four animals hiding in this sentence? Circle them.

Example: Help igloos!

Unfortunately, the intro utilizes expandable balloons.

57 Letter Scramble

Make four words using all of these letters: iedt.

1. _____

2. _____

3. _____

4. _____

58 Before and After

Put a word in the blank boxes so that it makes a word or short phrase with the word in front and the word after.

Example:

| S | P | E | L | L | I | N | G | | | H | I | V | E | = SPELLING BEE HIVE |

| H | A | I | R | | | B | A | L | L |

Word Box Challenge

59

Directions:

1. Find a partner.

2. You will each need a piece of paper and a pencil.

3. Each player draws a game board that looks like this:

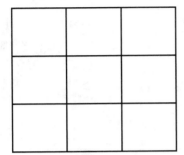

4. Take turns picking letters. You can pick any letter. You and your opponent should both write this letter on your game boards. Don't show your opponent where you put the letter! You can put this letter in any box. You need to include at least two (different) vowels.

5. Try to make three-letter words (vertically, horizontally, or diagonally; forward or backward).

6. Take turns picking letters until you have filled all nine boxes. Once you have filled all of your boxes, count your words.

7. The person who has made the most words wins!

   In this example, there are five words. Notice that *bat* counts as two because it can be read forward (*bat*) or backward (*tab*).

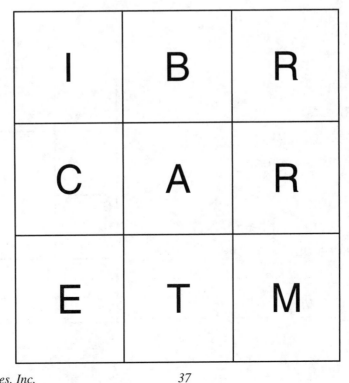

Hide and Seek

60

Can you find the three animals hiding in this sentence? Circle them.

Example: Help igloos!

Eggshell amassed makes the compost rich—it's not complicated!

Letter Scramble

61

Make four words using all of these letters: tsea.

1. _____

2. _____

3. _____

4. _____

Crossword

62

Read the clues and fill in the letters.

Across

1. A leaky faucet does this.
5. what you do on a horse
6. the opposite of *closed*
7. They are small, round, and green.

Down

1. to let something fall from your hand
2. a yellow banana (not a green one)
3. I have an _____!
4. You could use them to write.

1	2	3	4
5			
6			
7			

Hide and Seek

63

Can you find the three animals hiding in this sentence? Circle them.

Example: Help igloos!

The promo used a card in Alaska to ask unkind questions.

Letter Scramble

64

Make four words using all of these letters: psta.

1. _____

2. _____

3. _____

4. _____

Crack the Code

65

What has a head, a tail, four legs, and sees equally from both eyes? Fill in the blanks with these letters to find out!

e	i	s	a	n	h	d

	■	b	l			■	o	r	

Rhyme Game

Directions:

1. Find a partner. Each of you will need a copy of this sheet. Then, look at the words below.

2. Race to write rhymes for these words. Remember, words don't have to be spelled the same to rhyme!

3. Once you write three rhymes in a box, the box is closed.

4. Whoever closes the most boxes wins!

5. If you have time, work together to write a poem using some of these words.

start	teacher	float
rhyme 1: _____	rhyme 1: _____	rhyme 1: _____
rhyme 2: _____	rhyme 2: _____	rhyme 2: _____
rhyme 3: _____	rhyme 3: _____	rhyme 3: _____
luster	finger	bland
rhyme 1: _____	rhyme 1: _____	rhyme 1: _____
rhyme 2: _____	rhyme 2: _____	rhyme 2: _____
rhyme 3: _____	rhyme 3: _____	rhyme 3: _____
ache	lunch	handle
rhyme 1: _____	rhyme 1: _____	rhyme 1: _____
rhyme 2: _____	rhyme 2: _____	rhyme 2: _____
rhyme 3: _____	rhyme 3: _____	rhyme 3: _____
spring	board	tumble
rhyme 1: _____	rhyme 1: _____	rhyme 1: _____
rhyme 2: _____	rhyme 2: _____	rhyme 2: _____
rhyme 3: _____	rhyme 3: _____	rhyme 3: _____

Hide and Seek

67

Can you find the three animals hiding in this sentence? Circle them.

Example: Hel(p ig)loos!

To take the metro, utilize a thousand dollars (or take a different route).

Letter Scramble

68

Make three words using all of these letters: badr.

1. _____

2. _____

3. _____

Before and After

69

Put a word in the blank boxes so that it makes a word or short phrase with the words in front and the word after.

Example:

| S | P | E | L | L | I | N | G | | | H | I | V | E | = SPELLING BEE HIVE |

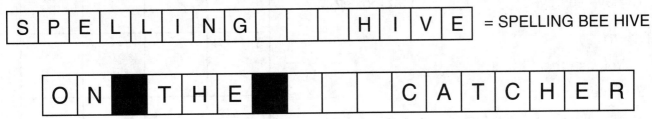

Letter Scramble

70

Make two words using all of these letters: crdewoh.

1. _Chowdir_

2. _cowhard_

Hide and Seek

71

Can you find the three animals hiding in this sentence? Circle them.

Example: Help igloos!

Most rich people would think it havoc to push subpar, rotting garbage.

Crossword

72

Read the clues and fill in the letters.

Across

1. the opposite of *first*
5. your voice, coming back
6. If you water a plant, it will _____.
7. Have you ever _____ that movie?

Down

1. You use them to run.
2. a measure of land
3. You wear it on your foot.
4. like a city, but smaller

1	2	3	4
5			
6			
7			

42

Crossword Challenge

Directions:

1. Using different-colored pens, work with a partner to put these words into the crossword puzzle. Each word must touch at least one other word.

2. Now, take turns adding new words to the puzzle. Be creative!

3. The person who can add the most new words wins.

4. Once you have finished the game, write clues for your answers. Make a crossword board with numbers that match your answers. Ask a friend to solve your crossword puzzle!

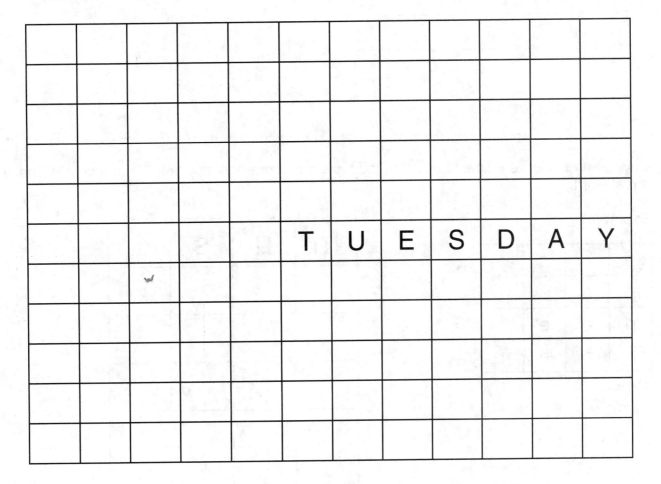

74 Hide and Seek

Can you find the five animals hiding in this sentence? Circle them.

Example: Hel(p ig)loos!

The face mask, unknown to Ratchel,
was part of an old, eerie replica train set.

75 Letter Scramble

Make three words using all of these letters: ainsl.

1. _____

2. _____

3. _____

76 Transformers

Change one letter at a time to get from the top word to the bottom word. Each row must make a real word.

Example:

p	e	s	t
p	**o**	s	t
p	o	**e**	t
p	o	e	**m**

m	u	s	t
s	i	l	o

Hide and Seek

77

Can you find the three animals hiding in this sentence? Circle them.

Example: Help igloos!

Catherine couldn't summon keystrokes to finish the proposal Monday.

Letter Scramble

78

Make four words using all of these letters: pslea.

1. _____   3. _____

2. _____   4. _____

Before and After

79

Put a word in the blank boxes so that it makes a word or short phrase with the word in front and the word after.

Example:

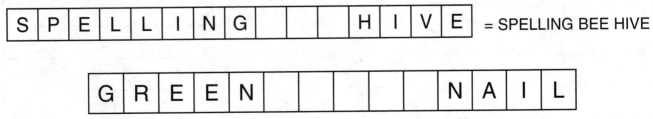

| S | P | E | L | L | I | N | G | | | H | I | V | E | = SPELLING BEE HIVE |

| G | R | E | E | N | | | | | N | A | I | L |

Fronts and Backs

80

Directions:

1. These letters are the "fronts" and "backs" of words.
2. Find a partner. Make a word using the "fronts" and "backs" provided. Write it in your space.
3. Take turns writing words.
4. If you cannot make a new word, you are out.
5. The person with the most words wins!

Fronts	Backs
mis	take
under	side
road	stand
with	out
hand	erly
form	less
un	some
awe	struck
	led
	way

Player #1	Player #2

Hide and Seek

81

Can you find the three animals hiding in this sentence? Circle them.

Example: Help igloos!

The larger billfold made the cowboy turn cartwheels.

Letter Scramble

82

Make three words using all of these letters: msae.

1. _____

2. _____

3. _____

Crossword

83

Read the clues and fill in the letters.

Across

   1. It has a shell and pinchers.

   5. to give someone a job

   6. I have an _____!

   7. the pointed top of a mountain

Down

   1. I love chocolate _____ cookies.

   2. The roller coaster is one.

   3. In a square, it is length times width.

   4. a bird's mouth

1	2	3	4
5			
6			
7			

84 Hide and Seek

Can you find the four animals hiding in this sentence? Circle them.

Example: Help igloos!

Costing Ray millions, the gizmo used chili on top of diamonds.

85 Letter Scramble

Make two words using all of these letters: bstea. As a bonus, make one more word!

1. _____

2. _____

Bonus: _____

86 Before and After

Put a word in the blank boxes so that it makes a word or short phrase with the word in front and the word after.

Example:

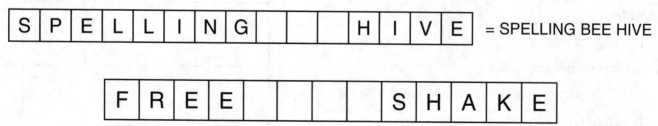

| S | P | E | L | L | I | N | G | | | H | I | V | E | = SPELLING BEE HIVE |

| F | R | E | E | | | S | H | A | K | E |

Beginnings and Ends Game

87

Directions:

1. Find a partner.

2. Look at the pictures below. Think of the words they show.

3. Start at *flea*. This word ends with the letter "a." Which word begins with the letter "a"? The first one has been done for you.

4. Take turns drawing arrows to the next picture. Also, write the words you use.

5. If you cannot find a word in 30 seconds, your partner wins. If you can use every picture, you both win!

Hide and Seek

88

Can you find the three animals hiding in this phrase? Circle them.

Example: Help igloos!

Wanted: One singer (bilingual) for pavilion show

Letter Scramble

89

Make four words using all of these letters: stkea.

1. _____   3. _____

2. _____   4. _____

Before and After

90

Put a word in the blank boxes so that it makes a word or short phrase with the word in front and the word after.

| C | E | I | L | I | N | G | ■ | | | F | A | R | E |

Crack the Code

91

What has fifty legs but can't walk? Fill in the blanks with these letters to find out!

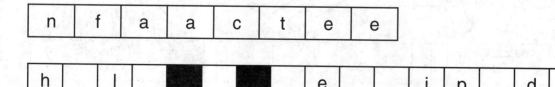

n	f	a	a	c	t	e	e

| h | | l | | ■ | | ■ | | e | | i | p | d | |

92 Hide and Seek

Can you find the five animals hiding in this sentence? Circle them.

Example: Help igloos!

"You can't eat erasers," scowled Frank in a nasal monotone.

93 Letter Scramble

Make five words using all of these letters: mtesa.

1. _____   4. _____

2. _____   5. _____

3. _____

94 Before and After

Put a word in the blank boxes so that it makes a word or short phrase with the word in front and the word after.

Example:

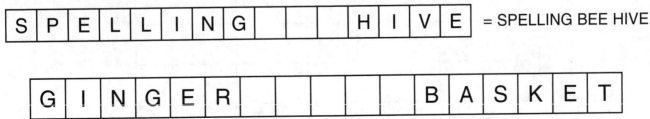

| S | P | E | L | L | I | N | G | | | H | I | V | E | = SPELLING BEE HIVE |

| G | I | N | G | E | R | | | | B | A | S | K | E | T |

95 Changing Letters

Directions:

1. Find a partner. Each of you will need a copy of this sheet.

2. One of you will pick a three-letter start word, and the other will pick a three-letter end word.

3. Write the start word at the top of your board. Then, have your partner write the end word at the bottom of your board.

4. Now, by changing one letter at a time, try to get from the start word to the end word. You cannot use a word more than once. You have five minutes to solve the puzzle.

5. The person who uses the least number of rows wins the round. If only one person solves the puzzle in five minutes, this person gets three points. If neither of you solve the puzzle, the round is a draw.

6. If you have time, play again. If you like, use four- or five-letter words by adding more rows and columns.

Example:

p	a	n
p	**i**	n
p	i	**g**
b	i	g

Start			
1.			
2.			
3.			
4.			
5.			
6.			
7.			
8.			
9.			
10.			
End			

Hide and Seek Challenge
96

The following places are hiding in the sentences below: Venice, Corinth, Malaga, Newark, Salamanca, Palmyra, China, Rome, and Athens. Can you find all of the places? Circle them. (*Hint:* There is only one place hidden in each sentence.)

A. Dismal Agatha's tooth aches.

B. We shall have nice cake for tea.

C. We have borne war; kings can do no more.

D. Eliza then said to me, "I have sprained my ankle."

E. After this refusal, a man called Anton popped the question.

F. March in a line.

G. I have lost my opal, my rather uncommon opal.

H. Will you be a hero mentor?

I. Do you like your poetry in the iambic or in the trochaic meter?

Crossword
97

This is a special crossword. The *across* words are the same as the *down* words.

Across and Down

1. You stand on it.

2. a type of dinosaur: veloci _____

3. to be against

4. a perfect world

5. more nosy

6. how you would describe a cloudy, rainy day

1	2	3	4	5	6
2					
3					
4					
5					
6					

98 Before and After

Put a word in the blank boxes so that it makes a word or short phrase with the word in front and the word after.

Example:

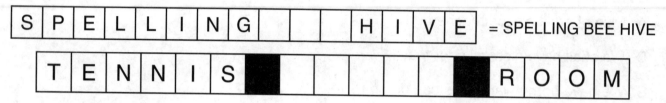

| S | P | E | L | L | I | N | G | | | H | I | V | E | = SPELLING BEE HIVE |

| T | E | N | N | I | S | ■ | | | | ■ | R | O | O | M |

99 Crack the Code

If we breathe oxygen during the day, what do we breathe at night? Fill in the blanks with these letters to find out!

| o | r | n | n | e |

| | i | t | | g | | |

100 Crossword

Read the clues and fill in the letters.

Across

1. If you are "it" in a game of tag, you _____ people.
6. Take it easy!
7. an excuse
8. They come before *tens*.
9. To win the race, Tom had to _____ himself.

Down

1. It lifts things to a building top.
2. The shape of DNA is a double _____.
3. The students waited in ____ _____.
4. A *Star Wars* sword is a light _____.
5. to be

1	2	3	4	5
6				
7				
8				
9				

54

Fill in the Blanks

101

Fill in the blanks to make this equation true.

$$\begin{array}{cccc} & \square & \square & 6 \\ + & 1 & 3 & \square \\ \hline & 4 & 9 & 4 \end{array}$$

In Addition

102

Fill in the blanks so that the sum of each row is the number to the right, and the sum of each column is the number below it.

12	17		8	53
	14	22	5	50
6	1			49
18		7	6	43

45	44	72	34

Sudoku

103

Each row, column, and 3 x 2 box has the numbers 1, 2, 3, 4, 5, and 6. Fill in the blanks to complete the puzzle.

	2	5	1		
			2		6
5	3	6	4		2
4		2	5	6	3
2		3			
		4	3	2	

It's Touching

104

Fill in the blank boxes with the numbers 1–5. Each full row and column contains the numbers 1, 2, 3, 4, and 5. Each shaded number is the sum of all the numbers touching it.

2	5	3		4
1	24		23	
3	4		1	5
	25	1	20	
4				2

Addition Tree

105

Put numbers in the boxes so that all of the boxes add up to the number they came from.

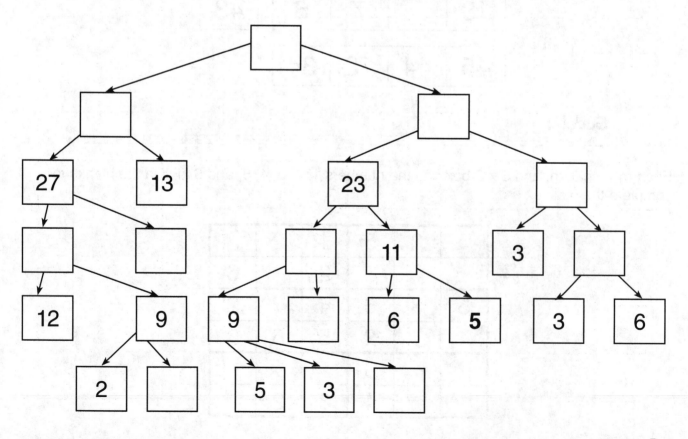

Snake Race

Directions:

1. Find a partner. Each player should use a different-colored pen.

2. Sit side by side, and put the game board in front of you.

3. Look for snakes that equal sixteen. The numbers have to be touching. (You cannot jump around.)

4. You may use a number more than once.

5. Start at the same time and race to find snakes. You get a point for every space you can circle, so a long snake is worth more than a short one.

6. After five minutes, add up your points. The person who has the most points wins!

Example:

3	+	1	+
+	8	+	12
8	+	4	+
+	9	+	9

Game Board:

34	÷	2	–	1	+	12	+	8	–
–	20	x	5	÷	4	–	9	+	5
24	–	16	x	2	+	6	x	2	x
+	4	+	28	÷	2	x	4	–	4
4	+	6	x	5	+	34	–	4	–
+	6	x	8	÷	3	x	2	+	2
2	x	2	+	5	+	9	÷	3	x
x	14	+	5	÷	11	–	2	÷	3
8	+	4	–	2	x	9	+	3	÷
+	4	+	4	+	9	–	90	+	6

107   Sudoku

Each row, column, and 3 x 2 box has the numbers 1, 2, 3, 4, 5, and 6. Fill in the blanks to complete the puzzle.

		1	5		
	5		4	6	
5	3	4	6		2
1		6	3	5	4
	1	3		4	
		5	1		

108   Thinking of a Number

I'm thinking of a four-digit number in which:

- the sum of the first two digits is fifteen.
- the sum of the last two digits is fifteen.
- the sum of the middle two digits is seventeen.
- the third digit is larger than the second.
- the last digit is an even number.

109   Math Path

Pick the best starting number, and then go up/down or left/right until you have touched all of the numbers once. What is the *highest* total you can calculate? Draw your path.

9	–	6
+	5	–
2	–	3

Total: _____

110 Thinking of a Number

I'm thinking of a four-digit number in which:

- the digits are in ascending order (with no skips).
- the sum of all digits is twenty-two.

111 Math Path

Pick the best starting number, and then go up/down or left/right until you have touched all of the numbers once. What is the *highest* total you can calculate? Draw your path.

15	–	5	+
–	6	+	9
2	–	4	–
–	3	–	5

Total: _____

112 In Addition

Fill in the blanks so that the sum of each row is the number to the right, and the sum of each column is the number below it.

8		4		9	**35**
5		9	14		**71**
9		23	3	15	**65**
		12	6	16	**63**
13	18		7		**75**
50	**88**	**64**	**35**	**72**	

Operations Game

113

Directions:

1. Find a partner. Each of you will need a copy of this sheet and a different-colored pen.
2. Look at the rows below. In each problem, you have to add, subtract, multiply, and/or divide to get from the first number to the last. The first one has been done for you.
3. Race your partner to solve the rows. You don't have to go in order. The person who solves the most rows wins.
4. Ready, set, go!

16	⊕ − / X ÷	4	+ − / X ⊘	5	⊕ − / X ÷	5	+ − / X ⊘	3	= 3
22	+ − / X ÷	11	+ − / X ÷	11	+ − / X ÷	12	+ − / X ÷	5	= 3
72	+ − / X ÷	12	+ − / X ÷	3	+ − / X ÷	9	+ − / X ÷	14	= 13
65	+ − / X ÷	27	+ − / X ÷	4	+ − / X ÷	5	+ − / X ÷	7	= 35
24	+ − / X ÷	12	+ − / X ÷	6	+ − / X ÷	3	+ − / X ÷	9	= 10
1	+ − / X ÷	15	+ − / X ÷	2	+ − / X ÷	3	+ − / X ÷	12	= 27
2	+ − / X ÷	3	+ − / X ÷	4	+ − / X ÷	5	+ − / X ÷	6	= 20
164	+ − / X ÷	4	+ − / X ÷	1	+ − / X ÷	4	+ − / X ÷	5	= 2
18	+ − / X ÷	12	+ − / X ÷	6	+ − / X ÷	6	+ − / X ÷	6	= 0

114 Fill in the Blanks

Fill in the blanks to make this equation true.

```
      6 □ □
  +  □ 3 9 6
  ─────────
    5 □ 7 4
```

115 Thinking of a Number

I'm thinking of a four-digit number in which:

- the difference between the first and second numbers is the same as the difference between the third and fourth.
- the sum of the first and second numbers is the fourth number.
- the difference between the second and third numbers is the first number.
- all of the numbers are even.

116 Sudoku

Each row, column, and 3 x 2 box has the numbers 1, 2, 3, 4, 5, and 6. Fill in the blanks to complete the puzzle.

	1	5	3		
		6			2
4		2	6	5	1
5	6	1	2		3
6			1		
		3	4	2	

It's Touching

Fill in the blank boxes with the numbers 1–5. Each full row and column contains the numbers 1, 2, 3, 4, and 5. Each shaded number is the sum of all the numbers touching it.

			1	2
	25		22	4
4	1	5	2	
	24	3	25	5
	3	2		

Addition Tree

Put numbers in boxes so that all of the boxes add up to the number they came from.

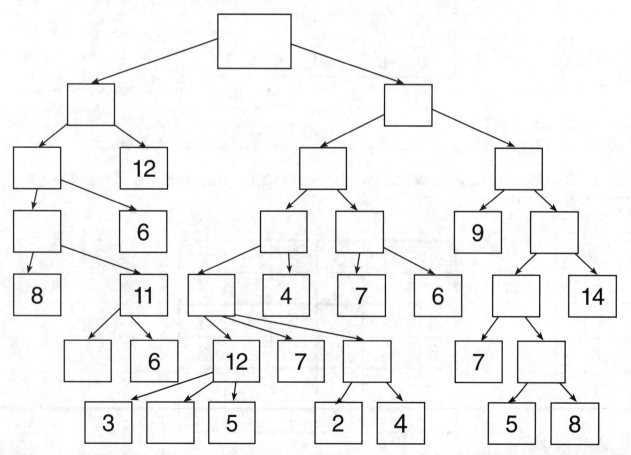

Addition Challenge
119

Directions:

1. Pick a colored pen. Have your partner pick a different color.

2. One player is on the left, and one player is on the right.

3. Look at the numbers in the middle. In each row, circle the numbers on your side that add up to the number in the middle. You can circle as many numbers as you need.
For example:

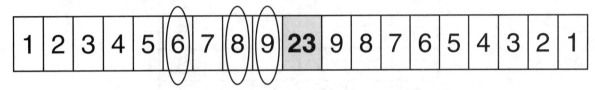

4. Once you have circled any combination of numbers, put an **X** on the number in the middle. That row is now closed. You get a point for each **X**.

5. Start at the same time and solve as many rows as you can before your partner.

6. You do not have to solve the rows in order. (You can start at the end or skip around.)

7. At the end, the person with the most points wins.

Player #1												Player #2									
1	2	3	4	5	6	7	8	9	10	11	**37**	11	10	9	8	7	6	5	4	3	2	1
1	3	5	7	9	11	13	15	17	19	21	**58**	21	19	17	15	13	11	9	7	5	3	1
1	4	7	10	13	16	19	22	25	28	31	**86**	31	28	25	22	19	16	13	10	7	4	1
1	5	9	13	17	21	25	29	33	37	41	**122**	41	37	33	29	25	21	17	13	9	5	1
1	6	11	16	21	26	31	36	41	46	51	**110**	51	46	41	36	31	26	21	16	11	6	1
1	7	13	19	25	31	37	43	49	55	61	**197**	61	55	49	43	37	31	25	19	13	7	1
1	8	15	22	29	36	43	50	57	64	71	**195**	71	64	57	50	43	36	29	22	15	8	1
1	9	17	25	33	41	49	57	65	73	81	**245**	81	73	65	57	49	41	33	25	17	9	1
1	10	19	28	37	46	55	64	73	82	91	**249**	91	82	73	64	55	46	37	28	19	10	1
1	11	21	31	41	51	61	71	81	91	99	**373**	99	91	81	71	61	51	41	31	21	11	1

Sudoku
120

Each row, column, and 3 x 2 box has the numbers 1, 2, 3, 4, 5, and 6. Fill in the blanks to complete the puzzle.

6		3	4	5	1
5			2		
4	3				2
1				4	5
		6			3
3	5	1	6		4

Thinking of a Number
121

I'm thinking of a four-digit number in which:

- there are two ways to get nine by adding some combination of these digits.
- the digits are in descending order, left-to-right (without any skips).

Math Path
122

Pick the best starting number, and then go up/down or left/right until you have touched all of the numbers once. What is the *highest* total you can calculate? Draw your path.

–	2	–	3
9	–	13	–
+	4	–	1
3	–	2	–

Total: _____

123 In Addition

Fill in the blanks so that the sum of each row is the number to the right, and the sum of each column is the number below it.

	13	22	90		164
54			19	21	124
44	12	19			153
	19	6	71	28	127
29		25		6	119
148	88	84	253	114	

124 Fill in the Blanks

Fill in the blanks to make this equation true. (Notice it is multiplication and not addition this time.)

$$
\begin{array}{r}
\square\,2\,3 \\
\times\quad 4\,\square \\
\hline
5\,\square\,\square\,1
\end{array}
$$

125 It's Touching

Fill in the blank boxes with the numbers 1–5. Each full row and column contains the numbers 1, 2, 3, 4, and 5. Each shaded number is the sum of all the numbers touching it.

	5	1	2	4
	26		25	
2	5			
	28		20	2
		2	4	1

Meet Your Match

Directions:

1. Find a partner. Each of you will need a copy of this sheet and a different-colored pen.

2. Look at the left and right sides in the columns below. On each side, there are equations that have the same answer.

3. Draw lines between equations that have the same answer.

4. The person who can draw the most lines wins.

12 x 12	5 x 39
7 x 16	6 x 24
9 x 22	1,346 − 912
155 ÷ 5	207 ÷ 9
184 ÷ 8	423 + 446
378 + 540	1,153 − 756
3,865 − 2,996	20 + 11
13 x 15	138 x 9
398 + 447	3,444 ÷ 6
62 x 7	28 x 4
634 − 237	27 x 34
54 x 23	11 x 18
14 x 41	924 − 79

Sudoku

127

Each row, column, and 3 x 2 box has the numbers 1, 2, 3, 4, 5, and 6. Fill in the blanks to complete the puzzle.

	5	6			
	2			5	4
		4	1		5
6		5	4		
1	4			3	
			2	4	

Multiplication Tree

128

Put numbers in the boxes so that all of the boxes multiply to the number they came from.

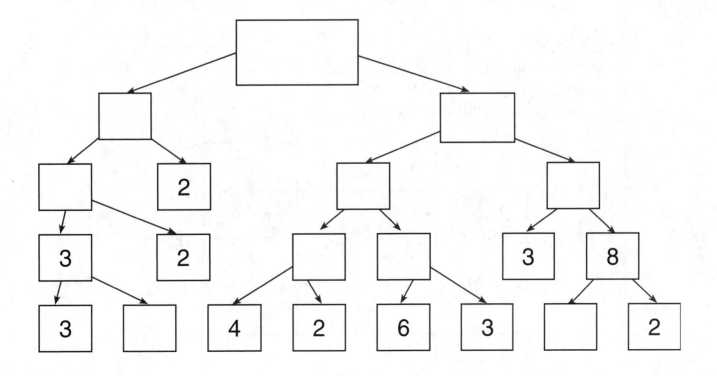

Fill in the Blanks

 129

Fill in the blanks to make this equation true. (Notice it is multiplication and not addition this time.)

$$
\begin{array}{r}
3\ 2\ \square \\
\times \qquad 2\ \square \\
\hline
7\ \square\ 1\ 6
\end{array}
$$

Thinking of a Number

130

I'm thinking of a four-digit number in which:

- the sum of the first and second numbers is six.
- the sum of the second and third numbers is seven.
- the sum of the third and fourth numbers is eight.
- the sum of the first and third numbers is nine.

Super Stumper: It's Touching

131

Fill in the blank boxes so that:

- each full row has the digits 1, 2, 3, 4, 5, 6, and 7.
- each full column has the digits 1, 2, 3, 4, and 5.
- each shaded number is the sum of all the numbers touching it.

5	6	1	3	2		4
2	28				35	
1	7		2	5		
			26			
3			2		6	

Tic-Tac-Toe Race

Directions:

1. Pick a colored pen. Have your partner pick a different color.

2. Choose a tic-tac-toe board, and sit side by side.

3. Start at the same time, and race to solve the math problems.

4. When you solve a problem, write the answer in the box.

5. If you get three in a row, you win.

6. Check your answers. If your opponent wrote a wrong answer, the space is yours!

Example:

6 – 4	4 + 2	8 – 3
9 + 5 14	4 + 5	2 + 7
1 + 6	3 + 9	7 – 5

Game Boards:

12 x 17	863 – 487	339 + 629
893 + 274	238 ÷ 17	24 x 27
321 – 292	84 ÷ 4	23 x 32

15 x 19	578 + 762	15 x 16
28 x 13	322 ÷ 14	789 – 487
734 – 729	42 x 6	124 ÷ 4

19 x 12	4 x 336	694 – 279
23 x 31	598 ÷ 23	378 – 279
37 x 24	984 – 884	15 x 62

346 – 287	498 + 279	16 x 23
592 – 465	984 ÷ 41	32 x 36
212 ÷ 53	13 x 15	92 x 6

133 Sudoku

Each row, column, and 3 x 3 box has the numbers 1, 2, 3, 4, 5, 6, 7, 8, and 9. Fill in the blanks to complete the puzzle.

	5	9		6	2	1		7
2		6		3		5	9	4
7	1	3		9			6	2
5		2		7	8		4	1
8			3	4	1			5
1	3		9	2		6		8
3	4					7	1	6
9	2	8		1		4		3
6		1		5		2	8	

134 In Addition

Fill in the blanks so that the sum of each row is the number to the right, and the sum of each column is the number below it.

12	18	8		27	77
21	17			32	96
9	12	26	11		63
4		9	8		35
		14	13	6	58
59	68	71	56	75	

Math Path
135

Pick the best starting number, and then go up/down or left/right until you have touched all of the numbers once. What is the *highest* total you can calculate? Draw your path.

2	–	1	+
–	4	–	7
6	+	3	–
–	2	–	3

Total: _____

Thinking of a Number
136

I'm thinking of a five-digit number in which:

- using any combination of digits, there are two ways to reach the sum of five and three ways to reach the sum of ten.
- the digits are in ascending order, left-to-right, but there might be skips.
- the sum of the first and last digits is seven.

Super Stumper: It's Touching
137

Fill in the boxes so that:

- each full row has the digits 1, 2, 3, 4, 5, 6, and 7.
- each full column has the digits 1, 2, 3, 4, and 5.
- each shaded number is the sum of all the numbers touching it.

	7			4	1	2
2	33			3	28	
1	6	5	3			
			6		1	

Snake Race
138

Directions:

1. Find a partner. Each player should use a different-colored pen.

2. Sit side by side, and put the game board in front of you.

3. Look for snakes that equal twenty-four. The numbers have to be touching. (You cannot jump around.)

4. You may use a number more than once.

5. Start at the same time, and race to find snakes. You get a point for every space you can circle, so a long snake is worth more than a short one.

6. After five minutes, add up your points. The person who has the most points wins!

Example:

5	+	7	+
+	8	+	12
7	+	4	+
+	9	+	6

Game Board:

2	+	5	x	2	+	8	x	4	÷
+	10	+	5	+	6	–	2	÷	2
5	x	3	x	2	+	6	+	5	+
x	2	+	7	+	1	x	4	x	8
3	x	12	+	2	x	2	x	3	x
+	15	–	5	÷	6	–	16	–	5
5	x	3	x	14	+	10	÷	11	–
x	6	–	1	–	6	x	4	+	4
7	–	4	+	7	+	12	+	6	x
+	11	x	2	–	16	+	15	–	4

Sudoku

139

Each row, column, and 3 x 3 box has the numbers 1, 2, 3, 4, 5, 6, 7, 8, and 9. Fill in the blanks to complete the puzzle.

5	6			9			2	
7		9	2			5	3	
		2		3	5		6	8
		4	8	2		6		3
	7						4	
3		1		5	4	7		
6	4		5	8		3		
	9	5			3	8		6
	3			7			5	2

Multiplication Tree

140

Put numbers in the boxes so that all of the boxes multiply to the number they came from. (*Hint:* A "?" means that there is exactly one digit missing.)

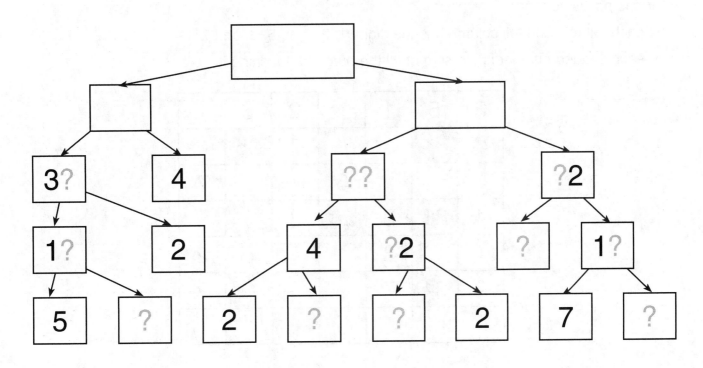

Sudoku
141

Each row, column, and 3 x 3 box has the numbers 1, 2, 3, 4, 5, 6, 7, 8, and 9. Fill in the blanks to complete the puzzle.

6				7		8	2	
5	3		6		2		1	
	7			1		3		
		7	9	6		2		
1	6						3	5
		4		2	3	7		
		3		5			9	
	1		2		9		4	8
	2	6		4				3

Super Stumper: It's Touching
142

Fill in the boxes so that:

- each full row and full column has the digits 1, 2, 3, 4, 5, 6, and 7.
- each shaded number is the sum of all the numbers touching it.

3	5	1		2	6	
				7	35	6
			6			7
4	28	2	28	3		
1		3				2
2	34	7				3
			5			

Target Number

143

Directions:

1. Find a partner. Each player should use a different-colored pen.

2. Take turns multiplying and dividing to try to get from one number to another. You may multiply or divide the number by any one-digit number (1–9).

3. Each player takes two turns at a time. After your partner has multiplied and divided the number, it is your turn. If you go off of the bottom of the board, draw your own spaces.

4. The person who reaches the target number wins!

Example:

Target Number: 12		
Starting # :		5
Player 1	x 6 =	30
	÷ 3 =	10
Player 2	÷ 5 =	2
	x 6 =	12

Target Number: 24		
Starting Number :		7
Player 1	=	
	=	
Player 2	=	
	=	
Player 1	=	
	=	
Player 2	=	
	=	

Target Number: 15		
Starting Number :		80
Player 1	=	
	=	
Player 2	=	
	=	
Player 1	=	
	=	
Player 2	=	
	=	

Target Number: 9		
Starting Number :		21
Player 1	=	
	=	
Player 2	=	
	=	
Player 1	=	
	=	
Player 2	=	
	=	

Target Number: 32		
Starting Number :		5
Player 1	=	
	=	
Player 2	=	
	=	
Player 1	=	
	=	
Player 2	=	
	=	

Target Number: 50		
Starting Number :		49
Player 1	=	
	=	
Player 2	=	
	=	
Player 1	=	
	=	
Player 2	=	
	=	

Thinking of a Number

144

I'm thinking of a five-digit number in which:

- by adding two or more of these digits, you can get the sums 4, 7, 14, 15, and 21.
- the digits are used only once (there are no repeats).
- the digits are in ascending order, left-to-right.

Math Path

145

Pick the best starting number, and then go up/down or left/right until you have touched all of the numbers once. What is the *highest* total you can calculate? Draw your path.

2	–	1	–
+	4	–	3
4	–	2	–
+	3	–	7

Total: _____

Sudoku

146

Each row, column, and 3 x 3 box has the numbers 1, 2, 3, 4, 5, 6, 7, 8, and 9. Fill in the blanks to complete the puzzle.

1			6				2	
3		2	1			6		8
		6	4		2		9	5
9		8	3					7
	6	7	9		5	3	1	
5					7	9		6
2	3		8		4	7		
7		1			6	8		4
	8				3			1

76

Sudoku
147

Each row, column, and 3 x 3 box has the numbers 1, 2, 3, 4, 5, 6, 7, 8, and 9. Fill in the blanks to complete the puzzle.

	5		1			3	9	
	7	2	8		9	5		1
	1	4		7				2
	4		6			2	5	
1			4		7			8
	6	9			3		1	
4				3		9	2	
5		1	9			2	4	7
	9	7			6		8	

In Addition
148

Fill in the blanks so that the sum of each row is the number to the right, and the sum of each column is the number below it.

7	14		56	2		92
25	16	9				77
		16	8	4		
11	12			14		94
7		21	3			105
83	63	82	123	87		

Prime Chase Race

149

Directions:

1. Find a partner. Each player should use a different-colored pen.

2. Look at the boxes below. In each box, you will be dividing by any number from 1 to 9 and keeping track of your answers.

3. During your turn, you can choose which box to work on. You can also choose any number between 1 and 9 to divide by.

4. In the example on the right, whoever wrote the prime number "5" scored a point.

5. Try to divide so that you can be the one to write the prime number.

6. Take turns until all of the boxes are completed. (You have to use your turn. You can't pass!) Once all of the boxes are finished, count to see who scored the most points.

Example:

Starting #:			2940
÷	7	=	420
÷	7	=	60
÷	6	=	10
÷	2	=	5
÷		=	
÷		=	
÷		=	

Starting #:			144
÷		=	
÷		=	
÷		=	
÷		=	
÷		=	
÷		=	
÷		=	

Starting #:			1008
÷		=	
÷		=	
÷		=	
÷		=	
÷		=	
÷		=	
÷		=	

Starting #:			720
÷		=	
÷		=	
÷		=	
÷		=	
÷		=	
÷		=	
÷		=	

Starting #:			945
÷		=	
÷		=	
÷		=	
÷		=	
÷		=	
÷		=	
÷		=	

Starting #:			4096
÷		=	
÷		=	
÷		=	
÷		=	
÷		=	
÷		=	
÷		=	

Starting #:			2448
÷		=	
÷		=	
÷		=	
÷		=	
÷		=	
÷		=	
÷		=	

Starting #:			176
÷		=	
÷		=	
÷		=	
÷		=	
÷		=	
÷		=	
÷		=	

Starting #:			2660
÷		=	
÷		=	
÷		=	
÷		=	
÷		=	
÷		=	
÷		=	

Starting #:			1840
÷		=	
÷		=	
÷		=	
÷		=	
÷		=	
÷		=	
÷		=	

Starting #:			2835
÷		=	
÷		=	
÷		=	
÷		=	
÷		=	
÷		=	
÷		=	

Starting #:			1872
÷		=	
÷		=	
÷		=	
÷		=	
÷		=	
÷		=	
÷		=	

Starting #:			384
÷		=	
÷		=	
÷		=	
÷		=	
÷		=	
÷		=	
÷		=	

78

Sudoku
150

Each row, column, and 3 x 3 box has the numbers 1, 2, 3, 4, 5, 6, 7, 8, and 9. Fill in the blanks to complete the puzzle.

4				2		8	1	
7		1	9				3	
6			3	1		7		
8	1		2		9		5	
	2						6	
	7		4		5		2	3
		5		9	4			2
	9				2	6		1
	4	8		3				9

Super Stumper: Multiplication Tree
151

Put numbers in the boxes so that all of the boxes multiply to the number they came from. (*Hint:* A "?" means that there is exactly one digit missing.)

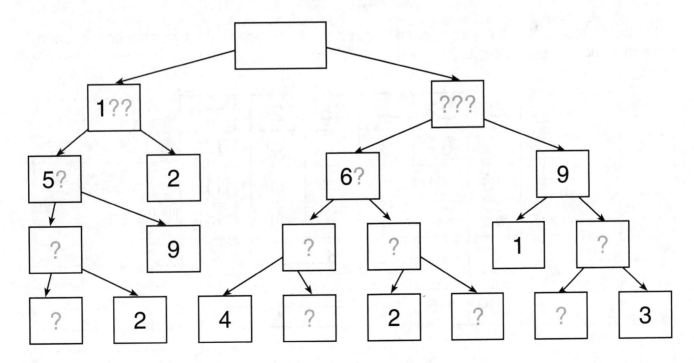

Sudoku
152

Each row, column, and 3 x 3 box has the numbers 1, 2, 3, 4, 5, 6, 7, 8, and 9. Fill in the blanks to complete the puzzle.

		4	5				9	
	8	5	3				4	
7			2	4		1		5
	4				5	9		
9		2	8		7	4		1
		1	9				6	
8		9		7	2			3
	2				6	5	7	
	1			9		2		

In Addition
153

Fill in the blanks so that the sum of each row is the number, to the right and the sum of each column is the number below it.

65	22		15	2	110
	61	3		52	147
48	29			11	110
63	1	5		41	115
7		12	6		41
209	116	28	51	119	

Fill in the Blanks

154

Fill in the blanks to make this equation true. (Notice it is multiplication and not addition this time.)

$$\begin{array}{r} \square\ \square\ \square \\ \times \qquad 3\ 1 \\ \hline 8\ 5\ \square\ 7 \end{array}$$

Super Stumper: It's Touching

155

Fill in the boxes so that:

- each full row has the digits 1, 2, 3, 4, and 5.
- each full column has the digits 1, 2, and 3.
- each shaded number is the sum of all the numbers touching it.

		2		1
	20		22	
1				

Sudoku

156

Each row, column, and 3 x 3 box has the numbers 1, 2, 3, 4, 5, 6, 7, 8, and 9. Fill in the blanks to complete the puzzle.

		9			2			5
	7	5		9			1	3
4				1	5		6	
8			2				3	
5		4	1		9	6		7
	1				8			2
	4		5	6				1
6	3			2		7	5	
9			8			3		

What's My Problem?

157

Directions:

1. Find a partner.
2. One of you is the Problem Master, and the other is the Guesser.
3. If you are the Problem Master, think of a two-step operation (like "double it and add two" or "add three and then multiply by three"). Do not use division. At first, make it easy.
4. If you are the Guesser, give the Problem Master a number. The Problem Master will start with your number, do his or her operation, and give you the answer. Try to guess the Problem Master's operation.
5. Mark your guesses and the answers in one of the charts below.
6. If you have time, switch roles and play again.

Guess Number	Answer

Guess Number	Answer

Guess Number	Answer

Guess Number	Answer

Guess Number	Answer

Guess Number	Answer

158 Fill in the Blanks

Fill in the blanks to make this equation true. (Notice it is multiplication and not addition this time.)

$$
\begin{array}{r}
5\ \square\ 6 \\
\times \quad \square\ 2 \\
\hline
\square\ 4\ 3\ \square
\end{array}
$$

159 Thinking of a Number

I'm thinking of a five-digit number in which:
- some combination of two digits adds up to four and five, but not six.
- some combination of two digits multiplies to three and four, but not five.
- some combination of two digits multiplies to forty-two.
- the order of digits (left-to-right) is largest, third-largest, smallest, second-smallest, and second-largest.

160 Math Path

Pick the best starting number, and then go up/down or left/right until you have touched all of the numbers once. What is the *highest* total you can calculate? Draw your path.

−	4	+	1
1	−	1	−
+	2	−	4
1	−	3	−

Total: _____

Mike, Anita, and Jamal

Mike, Anita, and Jamal ran a race and wore different kinds of shoes. Read each clue. Then, mark the chart to see who wore which shoes and which place that he or she finished in the race. The first clue has been marked for you.

Clues:

✔ The person who finished second wore slippers.

✔ Mike finished just in front of Anita.

✔ Jamal did not win the race.

✔ Mike did not wear sneakers.

Chart:

	1st	2nd	3rd	Sandals	Slippers	Sneakers
Mike						
Anita						
Jamal						
Sandals		X				
Slippers	X		X			
Sneakers		X				

Answers:

How did Mike finish the race? What type of shoes did he wear? _____

How did Anita finish the race? What type of shoes did she wear? _____

How did Jamal finish the race? What type of shoes did he wear? _____

What's Next?

162

Draw the shape that should come next.

◯▢△◯◯▢△◯▢△◯◯▢△◯▢△◯◯▢△◯▢△◯◯▢△◯▢△◯◯ ___

Apples and Oranges

163

If four oranges and three apples cost $4.50, and five oranges cost $4.50, how much does each piece of fruit cost individually?

_____

_____

_____

Letter Box

164

Put the letters A, B, C, D, E, F, G, H, and I in the boxes so that:

- reading clockwise around the outside, you can spell the words *bed* and *hag*, but these words are not touching. (There is at least one letter between these words.)

- a diagonal spells *ace*.

- F is above G and A.

- I is below D and E.

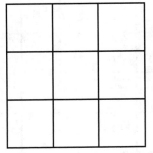

165 What's Next?

Draw the shape that should come next.

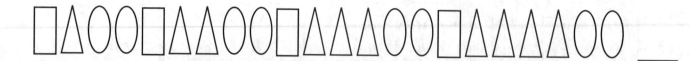

166 Paint by Numbers

The numbers along the top and side tell how many boxes are colored in. For example, if there is a "5," it means that there is a block of five black boxes somewhere in that row or column; if there are a "4" and a "2," there is a block of four black boxes and another block of two black boxes (separated by at least one blank box).

Color in the correct boxes to make a smiley face. Some boxes have been filled in for you.

						3	5	3			
					5	3	1	3	5		
			6	7	1	1	1	1	1	7	6
		3				■	■	■			
		5									
		9									
3	1	3									
		9									
	4	4									
2	3	2									
	2	2									
		7									

Mike, Anita, Jamal, and Kate

Mike, Anita, Jamal, and Kate live on the same block. Read each clue. Then, mark the chart to see who lives where and in which colored house.

Clues:

✔ Kate's house is farther down the block than Mike's. Neither Kate nor Mike lives in the blue house. Mike doesn't live in the green house.

✔ Anita does not live third or fourth, and she does not live next to Kate.

✔ The red house is first on the block, and it is not next to the green house.

✔ Jamal's house is the last house on the block.

Chart:

	1st	2nd	3rd	4th	Red	Blue	Green	Orange
Mike								
Anita								
Jamal								
Kate								
Red								
Blue								
Green								
Orange								

Answers:

Which house does Mike live in? What color is it? _____

Which house does Anita live in? What color is it? _____

Which house does Jamal live in? What color is it? _____

Which house does Kate live in? What color is it? _____

Connect the Dots

168

Can you connect all of these dots using only four straight lines? Once you start, you cannot lift up your pencil.

Apples and Oranges

169

If three apples and five oranges cost $5.80, and five apples and three oranges cost $5.40, how much does one of each cost?

_____

_____

_____

Letter Box

170

Put the letters A, B, C, D, E, F, G, H, and I in the boxes so that:

- the word *bag* is spelled horizontally (left-to-right), and the word *had* is spelled vertically (top-to-bottom).
- the vowels are all along the same diagonal.
- from top-to-bottom, one column reads E-B-F.

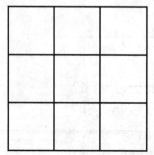

171   What's Next?

Draw the shape that should come next.

△ △ ○ △ △ ▢ △ △ ○ △ △ __

172   Paint by Numbers

The numbers along the top and side tell how many boxes are colored in. For example, if there is a "5," it means there is a block of five black boxes somewhere in that row or column; if there are a "4" and a "2," there is a block of four black boxes and another block of two black boxes (separated by at least one blank box).

Color in the correct boxes to make a monkey face. Some boxes have been filled in for you.

					5		5					
			1	1	2	8	2	1	1			
			8	8	8	8	1	1	1	8	8	8	8
		11											
2	3	2											
2	3	2											
		11											
		11											
4	1	4											
		11											
		11											
	2	2											
	2	2											
		7											

Racetrack

Directions:

1. Find a partner. You will each need a different-colored pen.

2. On the graph paper below (or another piece of graph paper), draw a racetrack similar to the one shown on the right. It can be any shape as long as it connects all the way around.

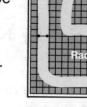

3. Pick a starting line, and decide on the direction of your race.

4. You will follow the lines (not the spaces!) to move around this track. Take turns moving your cars. The first person to get all the way around without crashing into the walls wins.

5. Here is how you move:

   • On your first move, you can go ONE SQUARE in any direction. Remember, you move along the lines, not in the spaces.

   • On your next move, you can go the same one square in the same direction, or (Get ready for the tricky part!) you can end your turn on any of the squares ONE SQUARE AWAY. Look at the picture to your right and imagine your move ended at the star—instead, you can choose to end at any of the circles.

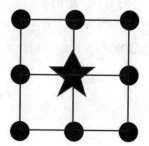

   • Draw your path!

   • On any move, you can go the same direction and distance as the move before.

   • By ending "one away," you can speed up, slow down, or turn. But you can't turn very fast, so be careful not to crash.

6. This sounds difficult, but once you learn how to play, it's really fun!

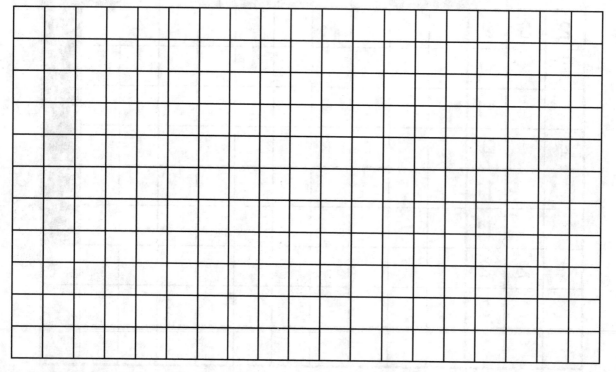

Jason's Hat

Jason lost his hat! Can you help him find it? Circle the correct hat.

Here are facts about Jason's hat:

✔ It has a striped band.

✔ It has one feather.

✔ The brim is only in the front.

Sprouts

175

Directions:

1. Find a partner. This game is tricky, so read the directions carefully!

2. Start with three dots on a piece of paper (like those given below).

3. Take turns moving. Each move has two parts:

   A. Draw a line connecting two dots (or a dot to itself). This line cannot cross any other line. No dot can have more than three lines coming out of it.

   B. Draw one new dot anywhere on your new line.

4. The winner is the last person who can make a move. Remember, once a dot has three lines coming out of it, it is blocked.

   Here is how a game might start:

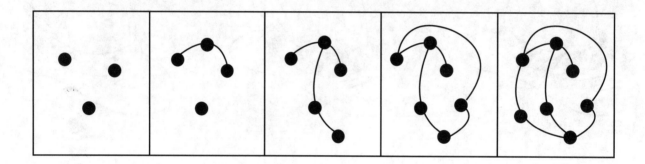

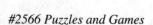

Melissa's Necklace

Melissa has lost her necklace. Can you help her find it?   Circle the correct necklace.

Here are facts about Melissa's necklace:

✔ It has large beads.

✔ It has a clasp.

✔ There is no pendant.

  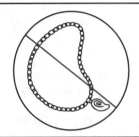

 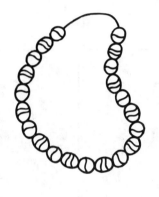 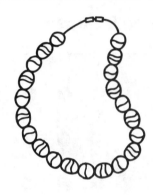

  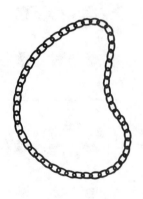

Boxed Out

Directions:

1. Find a partner. Each player should use a different-colored pen.

2. Look at the dots below.

3. Take turns drawing a short line between two dots.

4. Try to make closed boxes. When you make a box, color it in. Then, go again.

5. The person who makes the most boxes wins.

Example:

Game Boards:

Letter Box
178

Put the letters A, C, D, E, F, G, H, and I in the boxes so that:
- D, E, and G are in the same column, and none of these touch B.
- I, H, and G are in the same row, and none of these touch B.
- D, B, and F are in the same row.
- F, A, and H are in the same column.

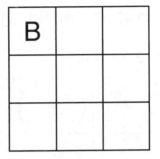

Paint by Numbers
179

The numbers along the top and side tell how many boxes are colored in. For example, if there is a "5," it means there is a block of five black boxes somewhere in that row or column; if there are a "4" and a "2," there is a block of four black boxes and another block of two black boxes (separated by at least one blank box).

Color in the correct boxes to make a fish. Some boxes have been filled in for you.

		6	4	2	4	5	6	6	6	3	5	3
										1		
1	4					■	■	■	■			
2	7											
8	2											
	11											
2	8											
1	5											

Hexagons Across!

Directions:

1. Find a partner. Each player should use a different-colored pen.
2. On one of the game boards below, take turns coloring in hexagons. During your turn, you can color in any hexagon on the board.
3. Your goal is to connect a line of hexagons all the way across the board. You can try to connect a line, or you can try to block your opponent.
4. The first person to connect a line all the way across wins.

Game Boards:

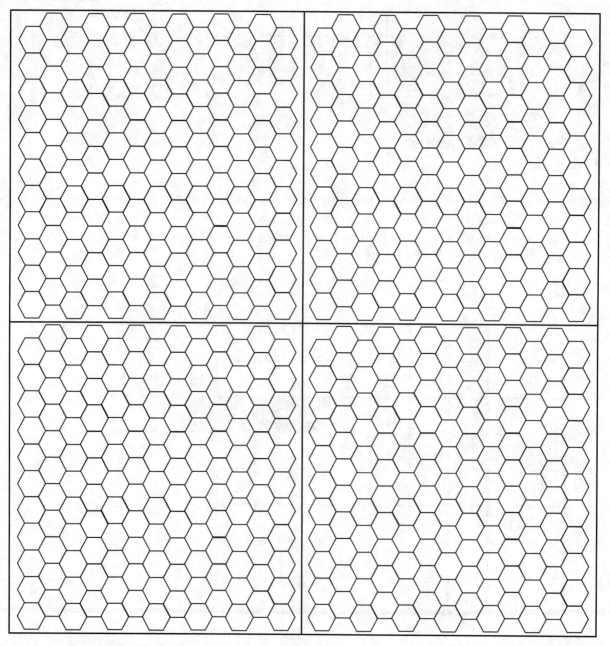

Mike, Anita, Jamal, and Kate

181

Mike, Anne, Jamal, and Kate have different pets. Each person also has a different height. Read each clue. Then, mark the chart to see who owns which pet and how tall each person is.

Clues:

✔ The shortest person owns a gerbil, and the tallest person owns a dog.

✔ Anita and Jamal are both taller than Kate, and Anita and Kate are both taller than Mike.

✔ Anita does not own a dog.

✔ The person who owns a cat is taller than the person who owns a bird.

Chart:

	Tallest	2nd Tallest	3rd Tallest	Shortest	Dog	Cat	Bird	Gerbil
Mike								
Anita								
Jamal								
Kate								
Dog								
Cat								
Bird								
Gerbil								

Answers:

Which pet does Mike own? What is his height compared to his friends? _____

Which pet does Anita own? What is her height compared to her friends? _____

Which pet does Jamal own? What is his height compared to his friends? _____

Which pet does Kate own? What is her height compared to her friends? _____

182 Letter Box

Put the letters A, D, E, G, H, and I in the boxes so that:

- all of the consonants are touching (no diagonals).
- all of the vowels are touching.
- the word *aid* appears either vertically, horizontally, or diagonally.
- G is not in the bottom row.

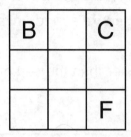

183 Paint by Numbers

The numbers along the top and side tell how many boxes are colored in. For example, if there is a "5," it means there is a block of five black boxes somewhere in that row or column; if there are a "4" and a "2," there is a block of four black boxes and another block of two black boxes (separated by at least one blank box).

Color in the correct boxes to make a sailboat. One box has been filled in for you.

								6	5	4	3
	2	2	2	3	3	4	12	3	2	2	2
1							■				
2											
3											
4											
5											
5											
5											
1											
11											
11											
5											
2											

Four-in-a-Line

Directions:

1. Find a partner. One of you is **X**s and the other is **O**s.
2. Look at the game boards below. Imagine you could drop an **X** or an **O** into the top of a game board, and it would fall down to the bottom.
3. Take turns "dropping" your letter. Mark your moves on the game board.
4. The first person to get his or her four letters in a row wins.
5. If you have time, play again!

Game Boards:

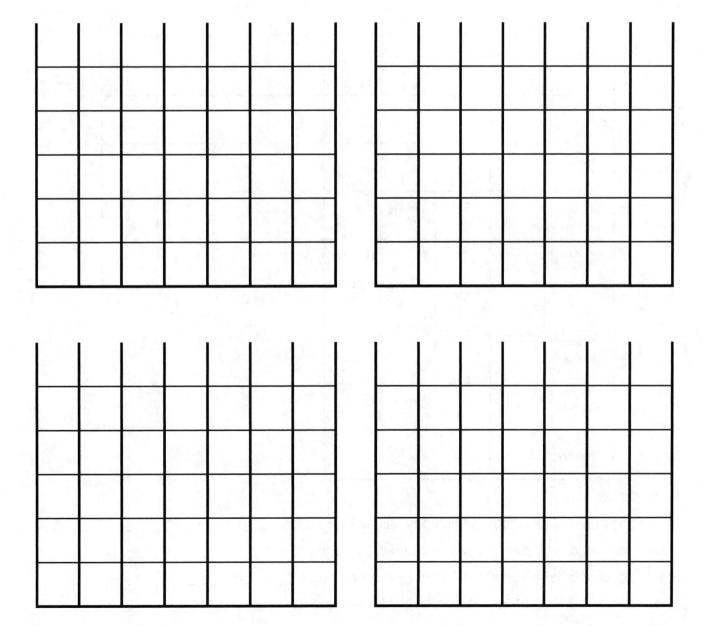

Mike, Anita, Jamal, and Kate

185

Mike, Anita, Jamal, and Kate each brought a snack for the class, one on each of the first four days of the school week. Among them, they brought carrots, crackers, rolls, and oranges. Read each clue. Then, mark the chart to see who bought which snack.

Clues:

✔ Rolls and carrots came earlier in the week than crackers and oranges.

✔ Mike did not bring rolls. Neither of the girls brought carrots.

✔ Jamal brought a snack on Monday, but it was not carrots.

✔ Anita brought a snack earlier in the week than Kate. Anita did not bring oranges.

Chart:

	Carrots	Crackers	Rolls	Oranges	Monday	Tuesday	Wednesday	Thursday
Mike								
Anita								
Jamal								
Kate								
Monday								
Tuesday								
Wednesday								
Thursday								

Answers:

Which snack did Mike bring? Which day did he bring it?_____

Which snack did Anita bring? Which day did she bring it? _____

Which snack did Jamal bring? Which day did he bring it?_____

Which snack did Kate bring? Which day did she bring it? _____

Five Sides

186

Directions:

1. Find a partner and choose a game board below.

2. Take turns drawing a straight line. Your goal is to make five-sided shapes (pentagons).

3. You earn a point for each pentagon shape you make. Keep a running total.

4. Each game has a five-minute time limit. At the end of five minutes, the person who has made the most pentagons wins!

Game Boards:

Example	Score
	Player #1 $\parallel$
	Player #2 $\parallel$

Game Board #1	Score
	Player #1
	Player #2

Game Board #2	Score
	Player #1
	Player #2

Game Board #3	Score
	Player #1
	Player #2

Answer Key

Note: Answers are organized according to puzzle number, not page number.

Picture Puzzles

1. I see you are too wise for me.
   paradise

2. thirty-two

3. Answer may be rotated.

5. Answer may be rotated.

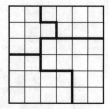

6. In the second picture, the boy has a cowlick, and his shirt has an extra stripe; the book is smaller, and there's a glass of milk on the desk; also, the dog looks surprised.

7. Your time is up.
   vacation overseas

8. Answers may vary.

9. twenty-one

11.

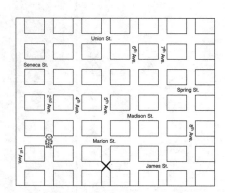

Answers may vary. *Bonus:* Go east on James St. Turn left on 8th Ave. End at the corner of 8th Ave. and Seneca St.

12. checkup
    domino

13. Answer may be rotated.

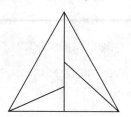

14.

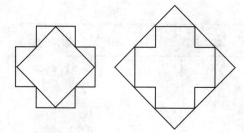

16.

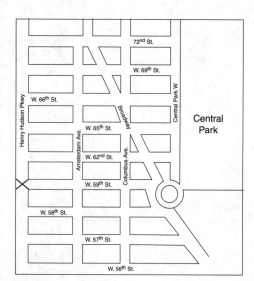

Answers may vary. *Bonus:* Go east on W. 59th St. Turn right on Columbus Ave. Turn left on W. 58th St. End at the corner of Broadway.

17. Answer may be rotated.

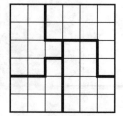

Answer Key *(cont.)*

18. In the second picture, there is an extra tree branch, and there are lines on the bark of the tree. The bird is missing, as well as one of the rocks, and the squirrel's ears are larger and tufted.

19. Answers may vary.

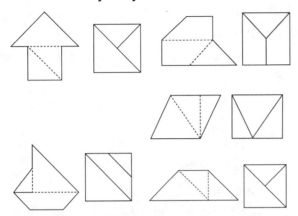

20. Answer may be rotated.

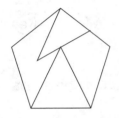

21.

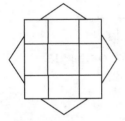

22. What goes up must come down. life of ease

23. Answer may be rotated.

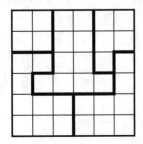

24. six

26.

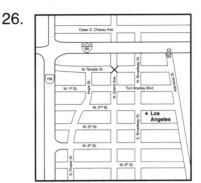

Answers may vary. *Bonus:* Go south on N. Grand Ave. Turn right on W. 5th St. End at the corner of W. 5th St. and S. Flower St.

27. makeup
   neon lights

28. Answer may be rotated.

29. In the second picture, the kite has no tail, there is more slack in the kite string (It's drooping.), there is another tree in the background, the girl is wearing sandals instead of being barefoot, and there's an airplane in the sky instead of birds.

31. Answer may be rotated.

32. six

33.

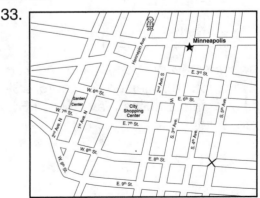

Answers may vary. *Bonus:* Go west on E. 8th St. Turn right on 1st Ave. N. End at the Garden Center.

Answer Key *(cont.)*

35.

36. twenty

37. sitting on top of the world
one in a million
Go for it.

38. toucans
highway overpass

39.
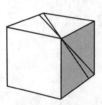

40. In the second picture, "Stairs" is written on the board instead of "Stars." The teacher has an extra pants pocket and a werewolf's hand. The piece of paper she was holding is gone. Also, one of the students is wearing a cowboy hat.

42.
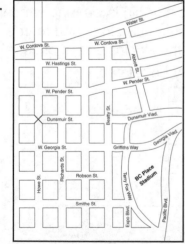

Answers may vary. *Bonus:* Go south on Howe St. Turn left on W. Georgia St. Continue onto Griffiths Way. End at BC Place Stadium.

43.
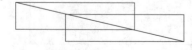

44. foreign language
horsing around

45. Answer may be rotated.

Word Puzzles

46. GRAND

47. Bingo attendance feels lugubrious tonight.

48.

¹t	²i	³l	⁴l
⁵i	d	e	a
⁶p	l	a	n
⁷s	e	n	d

49. cats, acts, scat, cast

50. We need a bigger billboard with the blob's terrible ooze branded on it.

51. a seasick tourist

53. Pro bingo players made lemon, Key lime pie for the fortunate cowboy.

54. nets, tens, sent, nest

55. Answers will vary but may be similar to:

n	e	s	t
n	**e**	**a**	**t**
m	**e**	**a**	**t**
m	e	a	l

56. Unfortunately, the intro utilizes expandable balloons.

57. edit, tied, tide, diet

58. PIN

60. Eggshell amassed makes the compost rich—it's not complicated!

61. eats, teas, east, seat

62.

¹d	²r	³i	⁴p
⁵r	i	d	e
⁶o	p	e	n
⁷p	e	a	s

63. The promo used a card in Alaska to ask unkind questions.

64. pats, past, spat, taps

Answer Key (cont.)

65. a blind horse
67. To take the metro, utilize a thousand dollars (or take a different route).
68. drab, bard, brad
69. FLY
70. chowder, cowherd
71. Most rich people would think it havoc to push subpar, rotting garbage.

72.

l	a	s	t
e	c	h	o
g	r	o	w
s	e	e	n

73.

						T	F
				W	H	R
				E	U	I
				D	R	D
				N	S	A
S			T	U	E	S	D	A	Y
U				S	A
N		M	O	N	D	A	Y
D				A
S	A	T	U	R	D	A	Y
Y

Other words will vary.

74. The face mask, unknown to Rachel, was part of an old, eerie replica train set.
75. slain, nails, snail
76. Answers will vary but may be similar to:

m	u	s	t
m	a	s	t
m	a	l	t
s	a	l	t
s	i	l	t
s	i	l	o

77. Catherine couldn't summon keystrokes to finish the proposal Monday.
78. pleas, pales, leaps, lapse
79. THUMB
80. Answers will vary but may include: mistake, miserly, misled, undertake, underside, understand, underway, roadside, roadless, roadway, withstand, without, handstand, handout, handless, handsome, handled, formerly, formless, unless, aweless, awesome, awestruck
81. The larger billfold made the cowboy turn cartwheels.
82. mesa, same, seam

83.

c	r	a	b
h	i	r	e
i	d	e	a
p	e	a	k

84. Costing Ray millions, the gizmo used chili on top of diamonds.
85. beast, beats
    Bonus: baste
86. HAND
87. Order may vary.
    flea → apple → elephant → tiger → rat → tooth → hand → dinosaur → raspberry → yak → kangaroo → orangutan
88. Wanted: One singer (bilingual) for pavilion show
89. stake, steak, skate, takes
90. FAN
91. half a centipede
92. "You can't eat erasers," scowled Frank in a nasal monotone.
93. teams, meats, steam, tames, mates
94. BREAD
96. A. Dismal Agatha's tooth aches.
    B. We shall have nice cake for tea.
    C. We have borne war; kings can do no more.
    D. Eliza then said to me, "I have sprained my ankle."
    E. After this refusal, a man called Anton popped the question.
    F. March in a line.
    G. I have lost my opal, my rather uncommon opal.
    H. Will you be a hero mentor?
    I. Do you like your poetry in the iambic or in the trochaic meter?

97.

¹g	²r	³o	⁴u	⁵n	⁶d
²r	a	p	t	o	r
³o	p	p	o	s	e
⁴u	t	o	p	i	a
⁵n	o	s	i	e	r
⁶d	r	e	a	r	y

98. ELBOW

99. nitrogen

100.

¹c	²h	³a	⁴s	⁵e
⁶r	e	l	a	x
⁷a	l	i	b	i
⁸n	i	n	e	s
⁹e	x	e	r	t

Number Puzzles

101.

```
    3 5 6
+   1 3 8
  -------
    4 9 4
```

102.

12	17	**16**	8	53
9	14	22	5	50
6	1	**27**	**15**	49
18	**12**	7	6	43
45	44	72	34	

103.

6	2	5	1	**3**	**4**
3	**4**	1	2	**5**	6
5	3	6	4	**1**	2
4	**1**	2	5	6	3
2	**5**	3	**6**	**4**	**1**
1	**6**	4	3	2	**5**

104.

2	5	3	**1**	4
1	24	**4**	23	**3**
3	4	**2**	1	5
5	25	1	20	**1**
4	**1**	**5**	**3**	2

105.

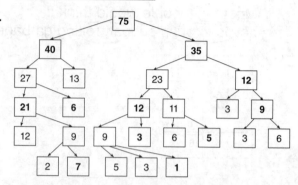

106. Answers will vary but may be similar to:

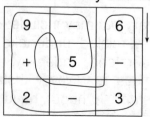

107.

4	**6**	1	5	**2**	**3**
3	5	**2**	4	6	**1**
5	3	4	6	**1**	2
1	**2**	6	3	5	4
6	1	3	**2**	4	**5**
2	4	5	1	**3**	**6**

108.

7	**8**	**9**	**6**

109. 5

Paths will vary but may be similar to:

Answer Key *(cont.)*

110.

4	5	6	7

111. 11

Paths will vary but may be similar to:

15	–	5	+
–	6	+	9
2	–	4	–
–	3	–	5

112.

8	**9**	4	**5**	9	35
5	**32**	9	14	**11**	71
9	**15**	23	3	15	65
15	**14**	12	6	16	63
13	18	**16**	7	**21**	75

50	88	64	35	72

113.

16 [+] [x]	4	5 [+] [x]	5	3	= 3
22 [+] [x]	11	11 [+]	12	5	= 3
72 [+]	12	3 [– x]	9 [+ –]	14	= 13
65 [+] [x]	27	4 [+] [x]	5 [+] [x]	7	= 35
24 [+] [x]	12	6 [x]	3	9	= 10
1 [x]	15	2 [– x]	3	12	= 27
2 [x]	3 [x]	4 [x]	5	6	= 20
164 [x ÷]	4	1	4 [÷]	5	= 2
18 [x]	12	6 [x]	6 [–]	6	= 0

114.

```
    6 [7] [8]
 + [4]  3  9  6
    5 [0]  7  4
```

115.

2	6	4	8

116.

2	1	5	3	6	4
3	4	6	5	1	2
4	3	2	6	5	1
5	6	1	2	4	3
6	2	4	1	3	5
1	5	3	4	2	6

117.

3	5	4	1	2
2	25	1	22	4
4	1	5	2	3
1	24	3	25	5
5	3	2	4	1

118.

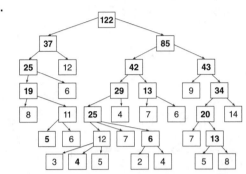

119. Answers will vary but may be similar to:

	Player #1														Player #2										
1	2	3	4	5	6	7	8	9	10	11	37		11	10	9	8	7	6	5	4	3	2	1
1	3	5	7	9	11	13	15	17	19	21	58		21	19	17	15	13	11	9	7	5	3	1
1	4	7	10	13	16	19	22	25	28	31	86		31	28	25	22	19	16	13	10	7	4	1
1	5	9	13	17	21	25	29	33	37	41	122		41	37	33	29	25	21	17	13	9	5	1
1	6	11	16	21	26	31	36	41	46	51	110		51	46	41	36	31	26	21	16	11	6	1
1	7	13	19	25	31	37	43	49	55	61	197		61	55	49	43	37	31	25	19	13	7	1
1	8	15	22	29	36	43	50	57	64	71	195		71	64	57	50	43	36	29	22	15	8	1
1	9	17	25	33	41	49	57	65	73	81	245		81	73	65	57	49	41	33	25	17	9	1
1	10	19	28	37	46	55	64	73	82	91	249		91	82	73	64	55	46	37	28	19	10	1
1	11	21	31	41	51	61	71	81	91	99	373		99	91	81	71	61	51	41	31	21	11	1

120.

6	**2**	3	4	5	1
5	**1**	**4**	2	**3**	**6**
4	3	**5**	1	**6**	2
1	**6**	**2**	**3**	4	5
2	**4**	6	**5**	**1**	3
3	5	1	6	**2**	4

121.

5	4	3	2

122. 7

Paths will vary but may be similar to:

–	2	–	3
9	–	13	–
+	4	–	1
3	–	2	–

Answer Key (cont.)

123.

18	13	22	90	**21**	164
54	**18**	**12**	19	21	124
44	12	19	**40**	**38**	153
3	19	6	71	28	127
29	**26**	25	**33**	6	119

148	88	84	253	114

124.

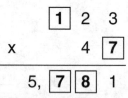

```
    1  2  3
x      4  7
─────────────
 5, 7  8  1
```

125.

3	5	1	2	4
1	26	**5**	25	**5**
2	5	4	1	3
4	28	**3**	20	2
5	3	2	4	1

126.

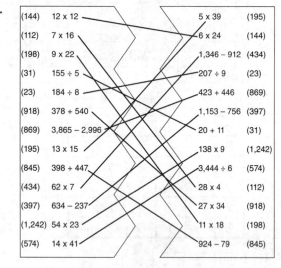

(144)	12 x 12		5 x 39	(195)
(112)	7 x 16		6 x 24	(144)
(198)	9 x 22		1,346 – 912	(434)
(31)	155 ÷ 5		207 ÷ 9	(23)
(23)	184 ÷ 8		423 + 446	(869)
(918)	378 + 540		1,153 – 756	(397)
(869)	3,865 – 2,996		20 + 11	(31)
(195)	13 x 15		138 x 9	(1,242)
(845)	398 + 447		3,444 ÷ 6	(574)
(434)	62 x 7		28 x 4	(112)
(397)	634 – 237		27 x 34	(918)
(1,242)	54 x 23		11 x 18	(198)
(574)	14 x 41		924 – 79	(845)

127.

4	5	6	3	1	2
3	2	1	6	5	4
2	3	4	1	6	5
6	1	5	4	2	3
1	4	2	5	3	6
5	6	3	2	4	1

128.

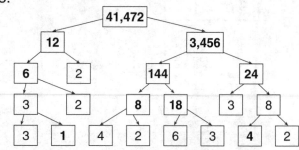

129.

```
     3  2  8
x       2  2
─────────────
  7, 2  1  6
```

130.

4	2	5	3

131.

5	6	1	3	2	**7**	4
2	28	**2**	22	**3**	35	**5**
1	7	4	2	5	**6**	3
4	34	**3**	26	**1**	28	2
3	**7**	5	2	4	6	1

132.

12 x 17	863 – 487	339 + 629	15 x 19	578 + 762	15 x 16
204	376	968	285	1,340	240
893 + 274	238 ÷ 17	24 x 27	28 x 13	322 ÷ 14	789 – 487
1,167	14	648	364	23	302
321 – 292	84 ÷ 4	23 x 32	734 – 729	42 x 6	124 ÷ 4
29	21	736	5	252	31

19 x 12	4 x 336	694 – 279	346 – 287	498 + 279	16 x 23
228	1,344	415	59	777	368
23 x 31	598 ÷ 23	378 – 279	592 – 465	984 ÷ 41	32 x 36
713	26	99	127	24	1,152
37 x 24	984 – 884	15 x 62	212 ÷ 53	13 x 15	92 x 6
888	100	930	4	195	552

133.

4	5	9	8	6	2	1	3	7
2	8	6	1	3	7	5	9	4
7	1	3	5	9	4	8	6	2
5	9	2	6	7	8	3	4	1
8	6	7	3	4	1	9	2	5
1	3	4	9	2	5	6	7	8
3	4	5	2	8	9	7	1	6
9	2	8	7	1	6	4	5	3
6	7	1	4	5	3	2	8	9

Answer Key (cont.)

134.

12	18	8	**12**	27		77
21	17	**14**	**12**	32		96
9	12	26	11	**5**		63
4	**9**	9	8	**5**		35
13	**12**	14	13	6		58

59	68	71	56	75

135. 6

Paths will vary but may be similar to:

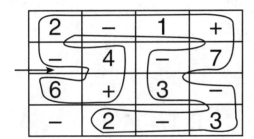

2	–	1	+
–	4	–	7
6	+	3	–
–	2	–	3

136.

1	**2**	**3**	**4**	**6**

137.

5	7	3	6	4	1	2
2	33	**4**	30	3	28	**5**
1	6	5	3	**2**	**7**	4
3	29	1	25	1	24	1
4	**7**	**2**	6	5	1	**3**

138. Answers will vary but may be similar to:

2	+	5	x	2	+	8	x	4	÷
+	10	+	5	+	6	–	2	÷	2
5	x	3	x	2	+	6	+	5	+
x	2	+	7	+	1	x	4	x	8
3	x	12	+	2	x	2	x	3	x
+	15	–	5	÷	6	–	16	–	5
5	x	3	x	14	+	10	÷	11	–
x	6	–	1	–	6	x	4	+	4
7	–	4	+	7	+	12	+	6	x
+	11	x	2	–	16	+	15	–	4

139.

5	6	3	4	9	8	1	2	7
7	8	9	2	6	1	5	3	4
4	1	2	7	3	5	9	6	8
9	5	4	8	2	7	6	1	3
8	7	6	3	1	9	2	4	5
3	2	1	6	5	4	7	8	9
6	4	7	5	8	2	3	9	1
2	9	5	1	4	3	8	7	6
1	3	8	9	7	6	4	5	2

140.

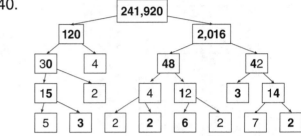

141.

6	4	1	3	7	5	8	2	9
5	3	8	6	9	2	4	1	7
2	7	9	8	1	4	3	5	6
3	5	7	9	6	1	2	8	4
1	6	2	4	8	7	9	3	5
8	9	4	5	2	3	7	6	1
4	8	3	7	5	6	1	9	2
7	1	5	2	3	9	6	4	8
9	2	6	1	4	8	5	7	3

142.

3	5	1	7	2	6	**4**
6	32	5	33	7	35	6
5	3	4	6	1	**2**	7
4	28	2	28	3	32	**5**
1	**6**	3	**4**	5	**7**	2
2	34	7	40	6	31	3
7	**2**	6	5	4	3	1

144.

1	**3**	**4**	**6**	**7**

145. 4

Paths will vary but may be similar to:

2	–	1	–
+	4	–	3
4	–	2	–
+	3	–	7

146.

1	5	9	6	7	8	4	2	3
3	4	2	1	5	9	6	7	8
8	7	6	4	3	2	1	9	5
9	2	8	3	6	1	5	4	7
4	6	7	9	8	5	3	1	2
5	1	3	2	4	7	9	8	6
2	3	5	8	1	4	7	6	9
7	9	1	5	2	6	8	3	4
6	8	4	7	9	3	2	5	1

147.

6	5	8	1	2	4	3	9	7
3	7	2	8	6	9	5	4	1
9	1	4	3	7	5	8	6	2
7	4	3	6	1	8	2	5	9
1	2	5	4	9	7	6	3	8
8	6	9	2	5	3	7	1	4
4	8	6	7	3	1	9	2	5
5	3	1	9	8	2	4	7	6
2	9	7	5	4	6	1	8	3

148.

7	14	13	56	2	92
25	16	9	22	5	77
33	9	16	8	4	70
11	12	23	34	14	94
7	12	21	3	62	105

83	63	82	123	87

150.

4	3	9	5	2	7	8	1	6
7	8	1	9	4	6	2	3	5
6	5	2	3	1	8	7	9	4
8	1	3	2	6	9	4	5	7
5	2	4	1	7	3	9	6	8
9	7	6	4	8	5	1	2	3
1	6	5	7	9	4	3	8	2
3	9	7	8	5	2	6	4	1
2	4	8	6	3	1	5	7	9

151.

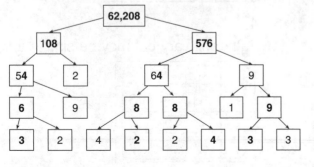

152.

2	3	4	7	5	1	8	9	6
1	8	5	3	6	9	7	4	2
7	9	6	2	4	8	1	3	5
3	4	8	6	1	5	9	2	7
9	6	2	8	3	7	4	5	1
5	7	1	9	2	4	3	6	8
8	5	9	4	7	2	6	1	3
4	2	3	1	8	6	5	7	9
6	1	7	5	9	3	2	8	4

153.

65	22	6	15	2	110
26	61	3	5	52	147
48	29	2	20	11	110
63	1	5	5	41	115
7	3	12	6	13	41

209	116	28	51	119

154.

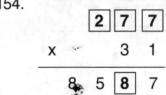

155.

3	4	2	5	1
2	20	1	22	3
1	4	3	5	2

156.

1	6	9	3	8	2	4	7	5
2	7	5	4	9	6	8	1	3
4	8	3	7	1	5	2	6	9
8	9	6	2	5	7	1	3	4
5	2	4	1	3	9	6	8	7
3	1	7	6	4	8	5	9	2
7	4	8	5	6	3	9	2	1
6	3	1	9	2	4	7	5	8
9	5	2	8	7	1	3	4	6

158.

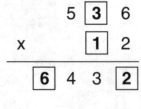

159.

7	4	1	3	6

Answer Key *(cont.)*

160. 3

Paths will vary but may be similar to:

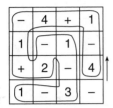

Logic Puzzles

161.

How did Mike finish the race? What type of shoes did he wear?
  first, sandals

How did Anita finish the race? What type of shoes did she wear?
  second, slippers

How did Jamal finish the race? What type of shoes did he wear?
  third, sneakers

162.

163. An apple costs $0.30, and an orange costs $0.90.

164.

F	B	E
G	C	D
A	H	I

165.

166.

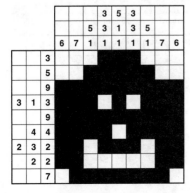

167.

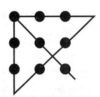

Which house does Mike live in? What color is it? second, orange

Which house does Anita live in? What color is it? first, red

Which house does Jamal live in? What color is it? fourth, blue

Which house does Kate live in? What color is it? third, green

168.

169. An apple costs $0.60, and an orange costs $0.80.

170.

E	H	C
B	A	G
F	D	I

171.

172.

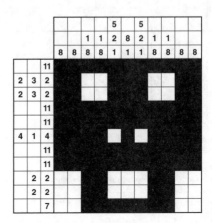

Answer Key (cont.)

174. Jason's hat has one feather, a striped band, and a brim that is only in the front.

176. Melissa's necklace has large beads and a clasp.

178.

B	F	D
C	A	E
I	H	G

179.

									1		
	6	4	2	4	5	6	6	6	3	5	3
1 4											
2 7											
8 2											
11											
2 8											
1 5											

181.

	Tallest	2nd Tallest	3rd Tallest	Shortest	Dog	Cat	Bird	Gerbil
Mike								
Anita								
Jamal								
Kate								
Dog								
Cat								
Bird								
Gerbil								

Which pet does Mike own? What is his height compared to his friends?
gerbil, shortest

Which pet does Anita own? What is her height compared to her friends?
cat, 2nd tallest

Which pet does Jamal own? What is his height compared to his friends?
dog, tallest

Which pet does Kate own? What is her height compared to her friends?
bird, 3rd tallest

182.

B	G	C
A	I	D
E	H	F

183.

								6	5	4	3
	2	2	2	3	3	4	12	3	2	2	2
1											
2											
3											
4											
5											
5											
5											
1											
11											
11											
5											
2											

185.

	Carrots	Crackers	Rolls	Oranges	Monday	Tuesday	Wednesday	Thursday
Mike								
Anita								
Jamal								
Kate								
Monday								
Tuesday								
Wednesday								
Thursday								

Which snack did Mike bring? Which day did he bring it?
carrots, Tuesday

Which snack did Anita bring? Which day did she bring it?
crackers, Wednesday

Which snack did Jamal bring? Which day did he bring it?
rolls, Monday

Which snack did Kate bring? Which day did she bring it?
oranges, Thursday